Secrets of traditional Portuguese cookery

The author

I. J. Lacerda was born in Lisbon-Portugal. He studied and worked as a journalist and interpreter in Germany and travelled in several countries of the World improving his knowledge of cookery and becoming serious about cooking.

After the experience of running his own bistros in Amsterdam and Lisbon he settled down in the Algarve-Portugal where he managed a restaurant for traditional Mediterranean-Atlantic delicatessen.

Currently he lives in the Algarve in the South-West Coast of Portugal and in Munich-Germany where he became an independent author. His books appear in different languages.

Other cook books

"The Mediterranean-Atlantic Diet"©2014 I. J. Lacerda
ISBN: 978 3 7357 1898 3
"Geheimnisse der lusitanischen Küche" ©2008 I. J. Lacerda
ISBN: 978 3 8370 9055 0
"Geheimnisse der portugiesischen Küche II" ©2011 I. J. Lacerda
ISBN: 978 3 8423 7108 8
"A Dieta Mediterrânica" ©2015 I. J. Lacerda
ISBN: 978 3 7347 6876 7
"Cozinha Medieval Portuguesa" ©2015 I. J. Lacerda
ISBN: 9 783 7347 6863 7

I. J. Lacerda

Secrets of traditional Portuguese cookery

(2nd Edition, revised)

Information der deutsche Nationalbibliothek
Die Deutsche Nationalbibliothek verzeichnet diese Publikation
in der Nationalbibliografie; detailliert bibliografischen Daten
sind in Internet über http://dnb.d-nb.de *abrufbar.*

A CIP catalogue record for this book is available from
Deutsche Nationalbibliothek in the National Bibliographical
Register in Internet at: http://dnb.d-nb.de

Copyright© 2015 I.J. Lacerda
Layout: I. J. Lacerda
Cover: Public domain
Herstellung und Verlag: Books on Demand GmbH, Norderstedt, Germany
ISBN: 978 3 7347 7321 1

Contents

FOREWORD 9
A SHORT HISTORY OF PORTUGUESE COOKERY 10
DAILY USES AND TASTES 11
HERBS AND SPICES 13
INGREDIENTS 14
QUANTITIES PER PERSON 14
STARTERS 15

Fried green and red peppers in olive oil 15
Eggs filled with curry paste 15
Home-made tuna paste 16
"Black and white" bean salad 16
Small mackerel pickled in marinade 17
Fresh summer salad 18
Runner bean salad 18
Algarve's small mackerel with lemon juice 19
Olives on herbs and garlic 19
Dates with Bacon 20
Cod fritters 20

SOUPS 21

South-West-Coast fish soup 21
Farmer's vegetable soup 22
Creamy chickpea and carrot soup 23
The friar's amazing "Stone Soup" 24
Creamy pumpkin soup with ginger 25
Tomato soup 26
South-West-Coast tomato soup 26
Gaspacho 27
Partridge-consommé with turnips 28
"Green Broth" or Caldo Verde 29
Chicken-consommé with rice 30

SEAFOOD 31

Lobster 31
Big crab salad 32
Fried prawns my way 33
Stewed seafood in the pan/Cataplana 34
Prawns and squid on the spit 36

Grilled king prawns 37
Clams Bulhão Pato 38

FISH *39*

Seafood or monkfish risotto 39
Grilled sardines 40
Mixed salad with green peppers 41
Northern-style trout with bacon 41
Grilled "Loup de mer" 42
Fisherman-style fish stew/Caldeirada 42
Fish broth with vermicelli 44
Fried small squid or cuttlefish 45
Spicy squid curry 46
Roast mackerel fillet 47
Roast sea bream with garlic and olive oil 48
Swordfish steak with onions 49
Tuna steaks with tomato sauce 50
Fried fish and tomato rice 51
Tomato rice 51
Roast eels with onions Franciscan-style 52

DRIED SALTED COD - BACALHAU *53*

Codfish with tomato sauce 53
Codfish with vegetables and egg 54
Gomes de Sá's codfish (in the oven) 55
Codfish with Port wine 56
Brás's codfish (with French fries) 57
Codfish my way (with cream) 58

POULTRY *59*

Goa-style chicken curry 59
Monchique-style chicken 60
(Home) fried potatoes 61
Romeo's grilled chicken 62
Braga-style roast (wild) duck with rice 63
Quails in Madeira sauce. 64
Crispy turkey with stuffing 65
Red cabbage with cumin 66

GAME *67*

Hare or (wild) rabbit (quick way) 67
The hunter's hare or (wild) rabbit 68
Stewed partridge with green peas purée 69
Fried partridge with mushrooms 70
Roasted pheasant with grapes 71

MEAT *73*

Plate of meat, vegetables and sausages 73
Red bean stew 74
Roast leg of pork 75
Stewed veal with wine 77
Noodles with pork 78
Beira-Alta-style pot-roasted goat or mutton 79
Pork loin with clams 80
Kid or Lamb stew with vegetables 82
Fried Pork loin cubes 83
Lisbon-style liver thin cutlet 84

STEAKS – BIFES *85*

Portuguese-style veal steak 86
Escalope of veal with Madeira wine sauce 87
Portuguese small pork cutlets/Bifanas 88

SIDE DISHES *89*

Green cabbage purée/Esparregado 89
Green pea purée 89
Carrot purée 90
Mashed potatoes 90
Garlic rice 90
Saffron rice 91
Grapes in Port wine syrup 91
Fried potatoes with cumin 92

SWEETS AND CONVENT DESSERTS *93*

Cherubim's pudding 93
Angel's cheeks – Papos-de-anjo 93
"Heaven's streaky bacon"/Toucinho do céu 94
Threads of egg yolk in sugar syrup 95
Milk pudding 95

Father Antonio's dessert 96
Special Christmas fritters 96
Golden Soup 97
Siricaia or Sericá 98
Sweet milk-rice 99
Pumpkin éclairs 99
Cream Pastries from Belém 100

SAUCES..101

White sauce 101
Cheese sauce 101
Butter sauce 102
Cocktail universal sauce 102
Farmer's sauce 103
Vinaigrette 103
Curry sauce 104
Butter sauce "Maître d'Hotel" 104
Tomato sauce 105

> If nothing said to the contrary all recipes serve 4
> Calorie counts are approximate values
> meant per serving

Foreword

Everyone who likes visiting or living in Portugal sooner or later will be interested in knowing something about traditional Portuguese cookery and the little secrets of its preparation. Eating and drinking are socially very important in the daily life of the Portuguese. A hearty meal with good wines can go some way towards improving friendships, business and politics. Discussing important plans over a good meal can lead to a successful outcome for all parties concerned. If a Portuguese invites you to a party, the party will undoubtedly be a feast!

In spite of over a million English speaking tourists visiting Portugal each year, very few books on Portuguese cookery can be found in their countries. Certainly many of those tourists long for a very special meal reminiscent of the ones they enjoyed during their visit to Portugal.

Portuguese cookery includes excellent fish and seafood dishes. It uses fresh fruit and vegetables produced by local farmers. Pork from Alentejo has a flavour all of its own (a result of the pigs feeding on acorns and truffles). Portuguese olive oil is one of the healthiest produced in Europe. The wine is for romantics and warms your soul. Portuguese cookery is versatile in its preparation and enables you to create delicious fish, seafood and meat dishes.

This book is a small collection of some of the best traditional recipes Portugal has to offer. Preparation is simplicity itself. Dishes can be created from a combination of ingredients which you may already have in your kitchen.

International cookery is drawing towards old fashioned home cooking. Portuguese cookery is the natural way of returning to this style, using seasonal ingredients.

I wish you a lot of pleasure in your cooking. "Bon appetite!"
I. J. Lacerda

A short history of Portuguese cookery

2000 years ago the Lusitanos as the Portuguese were called at the time were farmers and shepherds who fed themselves from the land by eating the vegetables they grew and the pigs and sheep which they reared. The Romans exported olive oil, wine and fish products *(garum - fish stock)* from the Iberian Peninsula. Later on, Gothic invaders introduced stews into the Iberian food culture. Southern Portugal has been influenced by the Moorish culture, which introduced a large variety of honey and almonds cakes, sweet rice and bread puddings were introduced by the Moors.

The discoveries of the 16th century brought to us, via Lisbon and Lagos in the Algarve, everything we know about exotic fruit and vegetables and spices. Cookery improved all over the country thanks to the rich nobility who had access to the best ingredients and the culinary skills which developed in many monasteries and convents. Nuns and friars collected many recipes from both home and abroad - they became the best cooks and confectioners. The farming population however, often had to sell the best of their own produce, which often left them with very little to eat themselves.

Amongst our specialities today you will find a great variety of puddings and fritters. Portuguese Jews created a sausage called *Alheira de Mirandela,* among other porkless products, which is a delicious garlic sausage made from venison and poultry. *Tempuras,* the Japanese fritters, were brought to Japan by Portuguese missionaries as a Lent tradition (the *temporas*). We introduced chilli peppers to Sichuan (Macau) and brought curries from India to Europe.

Around the 17th and 18th centuries the Portuguese nobility followed the French example of luxury. A "good meal" was an exotic banquet. Fantastic culinary excesses took place at the King's Vila Viçosa palace in Alentejo, costing a small fortune, and were an insult to the starving population. Portugal had to fight against serious political and economic crises. The population began to help themselves by growing their own food and breeding cattle of high quality. They followed the rule that good food came from their own farm or from the sea. Today you will find such quality at the local markets - fish from the coast is still delicious and home reared poultry remains a good choice.

Daily uses and tastes

Breakfast (Southerners call it ***pequeno almoço***, Northerners also ***almoço***).
The Portuguese will have a continental breakfast rather than an English one!

The extra bite taken about 11 am consists of an Italian espresso (***a bica***) and a piece of cake or a muffin.

Lunch (Southerners call it ***almoço***, Northerners ***jantar***) is served from 1 to 3 pm. Shops and offices close for two hours at lunch time. This is the time to sit and enjoy a complete meal.

Teatime or **the bite** between lunch and dinner (Southerners call it ***lanche***, Northerners ***merenda***) will be served about 5 pm.

Dinner (Southerners call it ***jantar***, Northerners ***ceia***).
Dinner it's similar to lunch; a three course meal is not unusual.

Snacks and unusual light meals (*the delicious petiscos*)
All over Portugal you will find wine bars (*tascas*) where you can eat snacks and light meals. Among such snacks and meals there is

a large choice of fish and meat pastries, cod croquettes, vegetable samosas or fritters. You may order a small pork (bifana) or beef steak (prego), fish fritters or roast pork (carne assada) served in bread rolls. Light meals such as minced chicken in a very hot sauce (pipis), fried partridge (codornizes), tripe with white beans (dobrada), octopus salad (salada de polvo) or snails (caracóis) are some of these unusual dishes which are served on small plates.

Country festivals and private parties (festas e romarias).
almost every town has a Saint's day. Over one or two days, people celebrate by going to markets, dances and eating! Depending on whether you travel to the north, middle or south of Portugal, you will find market places full of visitors and an aroma of fried chicken, roast suckling pig, grilled sardines and fritters.

Christmas and Easter also have their rituals. On Christmas Eve boiled cod with broccoli and eggs is a must. The next day relatives are invited to eat traditional stuffed turkey. At Easter Portuguese eat roast lamb and a cake (Folar da Páscoa) which has four whole eggs baked in its middle. On Easter day we offer one of these cakes to each of our godchildren. On St. Anthony, St. John and St. Peter's day (in June) there are great celebrations in Lisbon and Porto. People dance in the streets, eat grilled sardines and drink a lot of wine. On St. Martin's day (11th November) it is time for roasted chestnuts and tasting the year's new wine.

Traditional Mediterranean and Atlantic food
Traditional Atlantic cookery needs in its preparation more fish and seafood than meat, more potatoes than noodles, more olive oil than any other fat, more fruit than ready-made desserts and some good wine.

Herbs and spices

Before you start to cook Portuguese dishes there are certain herbs and spices which you should buy, as you will use them frequently. The list below is a guide to help you so you will have a good selection in stock.

- Bay leaves (*louro*)
- Cloves (*cravinho*)
- Coriander or cilantro (*coentros*) available fresh at Portuguese food markets and Asian grocers
- Curry (*caril*)
- Garlic cloves (*alho*)
- Ginger (*gengibre*)
- Gorse (*carqueja*) commonly use in venison dishes
- Oregano (oregão)
- Paprika (*colorau*)
- Paprika paste (*pimentão*)
- Parsley (salsa) use fresh flat leaf parsley
- Pepper (*pimenta*) whole peppercorns and ground
- Red chilli sauce (*Piri-piri*) such as Tabasco
- Rosemary (*alecrim*)
- Saffron (*açafrão*)
- Thyme (*tomilho*)

Tips

1. Some people love garlic. However, too much garlic can spoil a good meal. If not cooked properly, garlic can change a good sauce into a bitter one.

2. Too many bay leaves, or too much clove, aniseed, cinnamon or nutmeg will dominate a dish with their strong flavours!

Ingredients

1. Ingredients should maintain their natural flavour. The aroma of a dish should show the harmony between it's' ingredients and spices. Food should not taste too strongly of spices.

Quantities per Person

Soup:	1/4 litre/10 fl. oz.
Meat with bones:	150-200g/5½-7oz
Meat without bones:	100-150g/3½-5½oz
Mincemeat:	100-125g/3½-4½oz
Fish fillet:	150-200g/5½-7oz
Whole fish:	200-250g/7-9oz
Seafood:	200-300g/7-11oz
Shrimps and clams:	100-150g/3½-5½oz
Vegetables:	200-250g/7-9oz
Vegetables as salad:	100-150g/3½-5½oz
Pulses:	75g/2¾oz
Noodles and rice:	50g/1¾oz
Noodles and rice as a main course:	75g/2¾oz
Vermicelli:	15g/½oz
Potatoes:	150-200g/5½-7oz
Sauces:	3-4tbsp
Cheese as dessert:	50-75g/1¾-2¾oz
1 tbsp	5-15g/¼oz
1 glass	100ml/3½ fl. oz.
1 shot	½ dram
1 cup	8 tbsp./0.22 pint

To convert millilitres to fluid ounces multiply by **0.0351**
To convert grams to ounces multiply by **0.0353**
To convert kilograms to pounds multiply by **2.2046**

Starters

The following starters, except the ones made with eggs, may be kept in the refrigerator up to one week after preparation.

Fried green and red peppers in olive oil
Cal. 155

2 red and 2 green peppers, seeded and cut into small strips
Vegetable oil to fry
100ml/3½fl.oz. olive oil
1 tbsp tomato purée
Salt and pepper

1. Bring peppers to the boil for 10 - 12 minutes in salted water.
2. Drain peppers and stir fry in oil until just softened but not browned.
3. Add tomato purée, season with salt and pepper.
4. Place peppers in a terracotta pot and add olive oil. Serve cold.

Eggs filled with curry paste
Cal. 140

6 hard-boiled eggs, peeled and halved
1 tbsp olive oil
1 tsp curry powder
1 tsp chopped fresh parsley
3 black olives, stoned, cut into halves
salt and pepper

1. Carefully spoon the egg yolks into a bowl.
2. Add olive oil, curry powder and parsley to egg yolks and mix into a smooth paste. Season it with salt and pepper.
3. Spoon paste back into egg halves. Decorate each egg with half an olive. Serve on a small lettuce leaf.

Home-made tuna paste

Cal. 60

200g can tuna in oil, drained
1 tbsp leek, thinly sliced
1 tbsp cottage cheese
1 tbsp yoghurt
1 tbsp tomato ketchup
1 tsp vinegar
1 tbsp finely chopped parsley
Salt and pepper
Olives

1. Mix all the ingredients and mash well together with a fork, to make a paste.
2. Leave in the fridge for ½ hour.
3. Serve with bread and olives.

"Black and white" bean salad

Cal. 100

White beans with the small black "eye" are very popular in Portugal They are easy to prepare, requiring 5 -7 minutes in a pressure cooker, having first been soaked overnight.

250g/9oz beans, boiled and well drained
½ onion, finely chopped
Vinaigrette sauce to taste (see Sauces)
2 hard-boiled eggs, peeled and chopped
Salt and pepper
2 tbsp finely chopped parsley

1. Mix together the beans, onion and some parsley in a shallow bowl. Season it with vinaigrette.
2. Sprinkle the chopped egg over the top, season with salt and pepper to taste and garnish with parsley.

Reminder: Vinaigrette sauce is already salted!

Small mackerel pickled in marinade

Cal. 150 (2 small mackerel)

1kg/2½lb young mackerel
plain white flour, for dusting
175ml/6 fl. oz. vegetable oil, for frying
Salt

For the "escabeche" marinade:
2 carrots, cut into even-sized sticks
1 large onion, finely sliced
120ml/4fl.oz. olive oil, for frying
1liter/1½ pint white wine
8 tbsp white wine vinegar
1 tbsp whole peppercorns
5 bay leaves
1 tbsp roughly chopped fresh parsley
Salt and pepper

Tips to clean fish:
1. Clean fish by holding it firmly by the back. Hold the fish gills together and pull back to gut it. Rinse well and drain fish.
2. Place the flour in a polythene bag, then add the fish and shake to coat.

1. Clean and salt the fish, then dust with flour (see Tips above). Heat the oil and fry the fish until crispy on both sides. Place in a ceramic pot.
2. To make the escabeche: in a deep pan, stir fry the vegetables for about 5 minutes.
3. Add the white wine, vinegar, pepper corns, bay leaves and salt to taste; simmer for about 15 minutes. Add some more pepper and chopped parsley to taste.
4. Pour the marinade over the fish while still warm and set aside to cool. Leave to marinade in the fridge for several hours before serving. After two days marinating this dish tastes delicious!

Fresh summer salad

Cal. 210

4 hard-boiled eggs, peeled and sliced
4 tomatoes, sliced
1 garlic clove, finely chopped
Vinaigrette sauce (see109)
400g tuna in oil, drained and/or
400g pink peeled shrimps
Salt and pepper
Olives

1. Place in rows and layer on individual plate one egg, one tomato, a pinch of salt and pepper, a pinch of garlic, some tuna and/or shrimps and continue doing so until all ingredients have been used.
2. Season with vinaigrette and garnish with olives before serving.

Runner bean salad

Cal. 150

500g/1¼lb green beans, trimmed
Pinch of freshly grated nutmeg
1 tbsp smoked streaky bacon, chopped and fried
1 small onion, finely chopped
Vinaigrette sauce to taste (see Sauces)
Freshly ground pepper
2 hard-boiled eggs, peeled and sliced
1 tbsp chopped fresh parsley

1. Add a pinch of freshly grated nutmeg to salted water and bring to the boil. Add green beans and cook for about 7 minutes.
2. Mix the beans, onion and bacon in a shallow bowl and season with vinaigrette to taste.
3. Garnish with the sliced egg and some chopped parsley.

Algarve's small mackerel with lemon juice
Cal. 100 (2 small mackerel)

24 young mackerel, gutted (see p. 17, Tip)
Sea salt
Juice of 2 lemons
4 tbsp olive oil
3 tbsp white wine vinegar
2 carrots, cut into even-sized sticks
2 large onions, finely sliced
5 garlic cloves, finely sliced
2 tbsp roughly chopped fresh parsley
Pepper

1. Remove heads from fish.
2. Press each fish flat and season with sea salt. Place fish on a board, cover with another board and put some heavy weight on it. Leave to stand for 24 hours until the fish has lost its liquid.
3. Dip fish in cold water, skin it and carefully remove middle bone.
4. Place fish on a serving plate, season with lemon juice and garnish with onion and garlic.
5. Make the dressing by mixing together the olive oil, vinegar, parsley and pepper. Spoon it over fish. Serve with lemon wedges.

Olives on herbs and garlic

250g/9oz black olives
2 tbsp olive oil
2 small garlic cloves, finely chopped
1 tbsp dried oregano
Salt and pepper

1. Mix all spices with the olives in a bowl and leave to stand for at least an hour before serving. Serve with brown bread.

Dates with Bacon

Cal. 25 per date

16 large pitted dates
4 slices bacon
16 wooden toothpicks

1. Cut bacon in half, crosswise, and lengthwise.
2. Wrap each date with bacon. Fix each with a toothpick.
3. Bake in oven (200°C/400°F) until bacon is crisp. Turn once.
4. Drain on kitchen papers, and serve warm.

Cod fritters

Cal. 75 each fritter

150g/5½oz salted cod, soaked overnight, well rinsed
1 1/2 cups all-purpose flour
1 tbsp olive oil
1 teaspoon salt
1 1/4 cups milk
3 egg
2 tbsp parsley, finely chopped

1. Boil cod for 10 minutes, then drain, skin and bone then mash with a fork until coarsely fibrous.
2. In a large bowl, whisk together flour, olive oil, salt and pepper. Make a well in the centre and pour in the milk and eggs. Beat with an electric whisk until smooth.
3. Add cod, onion and parsley and mix well.
4. Heat olive oil in a deep frying pan. Use a ladle to put small portions of prepared mixture into pan and fry until golden.

Soups

South-West-Coast fish soup
Cal. 440

This is not the traditional fish stew "Caldeirada" (on p. 42).

5 x 120g/5oz slices sea bream, sea perch or sea bass
3 large onions, finely sliced
3 garlic cloves, finely sliced
300g/11oz tomato, peeled and chopped
100ml/3½fl.oz. olive oil
300g/11oz potatoes, peeled and finely diced
1 bay leaf
1 tbsp finely chopped fresh parsley
1 tbsp finely chopped fresh coriander
1 tsp oregano
Salt and pepper
4 slices brown bread, about 5mm/¼ inch thick

1. Stir fry the onion and garlic in olive oil (use a large pot) until just softened but not browned.
2. Add tomato, parsley, bay leaf and oregano. Season it with salt and pepper and leave to simmer gently. Add 2 litres/3½ pints water and bring to the boil.
3. Add the potato and fish, season to taste and cook for 15-20 minutes.
4. Carefully remove fish and set aside (use a fish slice or skimming ladle to avoid fish falling to pieces).
5. Place a slice of bread in each bowl and then add a piece of fish. Pour the soup over the fish and sprinkle with coriander.

Tip
If you wish to enjoy this as a meal, poach eggs in the soup after you have removed the fish. Add one poached egg to the fish in each bowl before sprinkling with coriander.

Farmer's vegetable soup

Cal. 270

Serves 6

500 g/1¼ lb potatoes, peeled and diced
2 large onions roughly diced
6 carrots, peeled and finely diced
500 g/1¼lb green beans, finely sliced
2 tomatoes, peeled and chopped
2 garlic cloves, sliced
100 g/5½ oz. butter (or margarine)
1 bay leaf
1 tsp thyme
1 tsp oregano
1 tbsp olive oil
Salt and pepper

1. Heat the margarine in a large pot. Add onions, garlic and bay leaf and fry until just softened but not browned.
2. Add the tomato and potatoes, plus 3½-4 pints of water. Bring to the boil for 20 minutes. Season it with salt and pepper.
3. Remove bay leaf, purée the soup until smooth. Add some water if the soup is too thick.
4. Add carrots, green beans, and remaining spices, season to taste and boil until the vegetables are tender.
Stir in the olive oil to add flavour.

Creamy chickpea and carrot soup
Cal. 130

250g/9oz chickpeas soaked overnight
4 medium size carrots, finely chopped
1 onion, spiked with 2 whole cloves
1 onion, finely chopped
1 tbsp olive oil
1 tsp curry powder
1 tsp Indian saffron
4 tsp cream to serve

1. Cook chickpeas together with the onion (in which you have inserted two cloves) in salted water, preferably in a pressure cooker, for 15-20 minutes.
2. Remove cloves and purée the soup. Add some warm water if it is too thick. Strain the soup through a sieve.
3. Heat oil in a large pan and stir fry chopped onion, carrot, curry powder and Indian saffron, making sure that the spices don't burn.
4. Add soup, season with salt to taste and simmer until the soup thickens slightly.
5. To serve swirl a teaspoon of cream into each bowl.

Tip
You may substitute spinach leaves for carrots if you prefer.

The friar's amazing "Stone Soup"

Cal. 490

There is a legend about this recipe, which shows how it came to have it`s odd name. The story is told as follows.

Once upon a time in Ribatejo (on the river Tagus area) a friar knocked at the door of a rich farmer and asked for something to eat. The farmer told him to go away as he had nothing for him. The friar then took a stone from his bag and told the farmer that he could cook a delicious soup with it providing the farmer could supply him with a large pan of water and a fire. The farmer was curious, and did not believe the friar, but asked him to cook this "miracle". He took him to the fire and gave him a large pan of water. The friar boiled the stone for several minutes, tasted the soup twice and then looked up with wonder at the large piece of smoked bacon that hung from the fireplace. He told the farmer that a small piece of the bacon would help the soup to taste must better. The farmer obliged and cut off a slice of the bacon, handing it to the friar. The friar added it to the soup, and after cooking it for a few more minutes tasted the soup again. He told the farmer it tasted very good, but... a piece of sausage and a carrot would really help to make it delicious. By continuing to do this, the friar duped the farmer into giving him all the ingredients he needed to make a delicious soup.

After eating, the friar took the stone, rinsed it carefully and put it back into his bag. This story has being told from generation to generation. All restaurants around the areas Almeirim and Santarém on the river Tagus cook the "Stone Soup". Even now, you should always remember to boil a little stone with the soup, otherwise the soup will not give the same result as the friar intended!

1 stone (take a round and smooth one!)
1 large slice of smoked streaky bacon
1 large potato, finely diced
1 onion, chopped
1 carrot, finely sliced
1 tomato, peeled and chopped
½ white cabbage, roughly shredded

100g/3½oz precooked brown beans
1 pork sausage
1 pig's trotter, well-trimmed!*
Salt* *A lot of Portuguese like pig's trotters and hog's ears. If you're not used to eating them, substitute with extra sausage (garlic sausage/chorizo, black pudding/morcela) or beef for them.*

1. Place the stone in a large pot, add 3½-4 pints of water and bring to the boil. Add bacon, trotter, sausages, onion, tomato and season lightly with salt (remember bacon and sausages are already salted). Cook ingredients until the meat is thoroughly cooked.
2. Take a small quantity of broth aside and purée half of the beans in it. Add the purée and remaining beans back to the soup.
3. Add potato, carrot and cabbage and simmer for 15 minutes until vegetables are tender.
4. Remove meat and sausage, cut into small pieces and place into bowls. Ladle vegetables and soup over meat and serve.

Creamy pumpkin soup with ginger
Cal. 225

500g/1¼lb pumpkin wedge, peeled and diced
1 large onion, chopped
1 leek, finely sliced
50g/1¾oz butter
4 carrots, finely sliced
2 tbsp freshly grated ginger
250ml milk
1 cup cream
salt and pepper

1. Melt butter in a pot. Add onion and leek and fry gently. Add pumpkin, carrot, milk, water and ginger. Season with salt and pepper, bring to the boil, then cover and simmer for 30 minutes. Purée the soup until smooth.
2. Stir in the cream, heat through gently without boiling. Add salt and pepper to taste.
3. Garnish with croutons and serve.

Tomato soup

Cal. 200

1kg/2½lb tomatoes, peeled and chopped
2 onions, chopped
2 potatoes, sliced
1 tbsp olive oil
1 garlic clove, crushed
1 bay leaf
pinch oregano
salt and pepper
cream
1 tbsp chopped fresh parsley

1. Heat the oil in a pot and stir fry onion, garlic and bay leaf.
2. Add potatoes and stir in the tomato. Season it with salt and pepper. Add oregano and water. Bring to the boil, then cover and simmer for 30 minutes.
3. Remove bay leaf and purée the soup.
4. Ladle soup in bowls, stir in the cream, add some croutons and sprinkle with parsley to serve.

Tip
If using canned tomatoes, add 1 tsp sugar before boiling.

South-West-Coast tomato soup

Cal. 270

1. Prepare soup as above.
2. Place some sliced brown bread in soup bowl. Ladle soup over the bread, then cover and keep it warm.
3. Add a poached egg to the soup.

Tip
In some regions this soup is served with fresh plums or figs.

Gaspacho
Cal. 170

This cold soup is probably inherited from the Moors living at the Peninsula. In the past it was prepared and eaten by farmers working in the fields, who could not spare the time to return home for lunch. Today it is still a delicious soup, served in Alentejo and Algarve restaurants, especially during the hot summer months.

500g/1¼lb tomatoes, peeled, seeded and finely chopped
½ cucumber, peeled and finely chopped
1 green pepper, seeded and finely diced
3 garlic cloves
250ml chilled water
3 tbsp olive oil
1 tbsp wine vinegar
1 tbsp chopped fresh coriander
pinch oregano
salt and pepper
100g/3½oz black olives

1. Purée half of vegetables with the garlic, water, olive oil and coriander.
2. Season with salt and pepper. Place in the fridge.
3. Mix remaining vegetables before serving into the purée and sprinkle with oregano.
4. Serve with bread and olives.

Tip
The purée can be served separately if you prefer. Season the vegetables with just a pinch of salt.

Partridge-consommé with turnips

Cal. 200

2 partridges, ready to cook
1.5 l/2½ pints water
1 tbsp olive oil
100g/3½oz smoked streaky bacon, chopped
1 onion, finely chopped
A dash of white wine
1 carrot, finely sliced
Small bunch parsley
Salt and pepper
1 bay leaf
2 turnips, peeled and cut into even-sized sticks
croutons to serve

Tip
Bone the partridge. Keep the breasts for another dish (p. 72) and use the bones for game stock. Use the rest for the consommé.

1. Place game, bacon, onion, carrot, parsley and bay leaf in water <u>without salt</u>. Bring to the boil. Season with pepper, olive oil and wine, then cover and gently simmer for about an hour. Remove meat and keep aside, simmer soup for another hour.
2. Strain the soup.
3. Cook the turnip in the soup for 15 minutes. Season it with salt and add the partridge meat.
4. Add small pieces of cooked breast meat to consommé if you wish.
5. Serve with croutons.

"Green Broth" or Caldo Verde
Cal. 135

Portuguese prepare this soup using a green cabbage called "couve portuguesa" (or Galicia cabbage) which has big leaves and is about 40 inches high. The large outside leaves are used, and then the plant is left to continue growing. You will probably choose to use a Savoy cabbage. The cabbage needs to be cut into very fine shreds - in Portugal you can buy them ready to cook! You will have to practice doing it yourself - roll some cabbage leaves tightly together and use a sharp knife to cut off very thin shreds. Mind your fingers!

500g/1½lb potatoes, peeled and diced
250g/9oz green cabbage finely shredded as above
2 garlic cloves, sliced
1 freshly ground clove
1 large onion, chopped
2 tbsp olive oil
Salt and pepper
1 garlic/paprika sausage or a Portuguese *"paio"*

1. Bring a pan of water to the boil. Add all ingredients and spices except the cabbage and sausage. Simmer for 20 minutes.
2. Purée the soup in a food processor (if you have one). Add cabbage and simmer for a further 20 minutes.
3. Spoon into bowls and add 2 slices of sausage to each bowl.
4. Serve with brown bread and black olives.

Chicken-consommé with rice

Cal. 220

This soup is known amongst the older generation as a household medicine, which will defend against minor illnesses and flu! Its ingredients include a freshly butchered hen (if possible) complete with livers and egg yolks!

1 fresh hen or 1 chicken, skinned, cut into 8 pieces
3 l/ 5 pints water
1 chicken liver
2 carrots cut into even-sized sticks
2 tbsp precooked rice
salt
mint sprigs, to serve

1. Cook the hen or chicken pieces and carrots in lightly salted water until meat comes off the bones easily. Remove any froth with a skimming ladle.
2. Put the meat and livers aside, discard all of the bones. Cut meat into small pieces and keep warm.
3. Strain 1.5 litres/2½ pints of broth. Cook the rice and egg yolk for 5 minutes in the broth. Season it with salt to taste.
4. Pour into bowls. Add meat pieces and sprigs of mint to each bowl.

Tips
1. You may substitute a beaten egg yolk with a pinch of plain flour for the fresh yolks. Add it slowly to the simmering soup.
2. Strain and freeze any left-over broth and use it later as poultry stock. Make note on the freezer label that the stock is already salted.

Seafood

Lobster

There are some important rules to follow when preparing shellfish.
a) Buy the freshest lobster available, preferably live.
b) A 500g/1¼lb lobster needs 15-20 minutes to cook.
c) Cook lobster in a Court-Bouillon.
d) Cut off the fine digestive cord on the back and remove the stomach sack. Both taste quite bitter.

1 lobster
175g/6oz butter
3 tbsp white wine
3 egg yolks
salt and pepper
some lettuce leaves

1. Drop the lobster in boiling "Court-Bouillon" (see next page) and cook for 15-20 minutes. Turn heat off and let the lobster cool down in the "Court-Bouillon" stock.
2. Clarify butter by gently heating. Stir into the water and wine, the clarified butter and heat gently until it thickens slightly. Stir egg yolks in a *Bain Marie* until doubles. Add butter and season with salt and pepper.
3. Remove legs and claws and break claws with a wooden hammer. Cut the lobster along into halves and remove the fine digestive cord and stomach using a heavy knife. Remove flesh carefully and cut it into slices of about 2cm/0.4in each. Arrange slices back into the shells.
4. Place both shells on lettuce leaves. Serve with the sauce and toasted bread, cut into triangles.

How to prepare a Court-Bouillon: 1 onion, 1 carrot, peeled, 1 bay leaf, 1 small bunch parsley, 1 handful sea salt, 1 tsp pepper corns. *Cook all spices in water for 10 minutes.*

Big crab salad

Buy the freshest crab available, preferably a live one. If it feels too light for its size then it' is probably empty. If you're not confident in choosing a good crab, ask the fishmonger to do it for you.

1kg/2½lb live or freshly cooked crab in the shell
1 small onion, finely chopped
1 tbsp mixed pickles, finely chopped
1 hard-boiled egg, finely chopped
50g/1¾oz black olives, stoned and finely chopped
Piri-piri or Tabasco
2 tbsp mayonnaise
1 tsp Port wine
small bunch parsley, finely chopped
Sea salt
1 lemon, cut into wedges to serve

1. Cook the crab in Court-Bouillon (see above) for about 20 minutes. Remove the crab and let it cool down.
2. Place the crab on a chopping board and remove the tail-flap, push the body, with the legs and claws still attached, away from the shell and remove the stomach sack and feathery gills (a grey-yellowish substance). Spoon all the rest out, chop it finely and put into a bowl. Set shell aside.
3. Mix flesh with all ingredients and spices. Spoon it back into the shell.
4. Garnish shell with legs and broken claws and serve with lemon wedges and toasted bread, cut into triangles. Serve immediately.

Fried prawns my way
Cal. 475

Raw frozen shrimps (gamba type) or king prawns are a good type to use in this dish. Don't use basic pink peeled shrimps as they will not work.

500g/1¼lb shrimps (see note about prawns on page 37)
1 onion, finely chopped
200g/7oz butter
3 tbsp vegetable oil
5 garlic cloves, finely sliced
2 tbsp Piri-piri or Tabasco
½ glass Brandy
½ glass Port wine
2 lemons cut into wedges to serve
sea salt

1. Heat half of the butter and the 3 tbsp oil in a frying pan. Stir fry the frozen shrimps until they change colour on both sides, then season them well with salt and Piri-piri or Tabasco or a similar hot sauce.
2. Remove frying pan from the heat, pour over the Brandy, bring it back to the heat and carefully ignite. When the flames have died down add the garlic and onion and stir well for 1 minute. Remove shrimps and set aside.
3. Add Port wine and rest of the butter to the sauce. Stir well to incorporate any sediment from the bottom into the sauce. Let it bubble for a moment then put the sauce through a sieve, over the shrimps.
4. Serve with lemon wedges and toasted bread cut into triangles.

Tip
As shrimps are eaten with your fingers, provide a finger bowl with warm water and some lemon slices.

Stewed seafood in the pan/Cataplana

Cal. 480

For the preparation of this dish there are special copper pans with a lid called cataplanas. They are used in the Algarve and available in different sizes (2,4,and 6). according to the number of people you are serving.

Tips
1. You may use any mixed seafood or just shrimps, clams, fish, etc. or even meat as main ingredient for the *cataplana*.
2. If you don't have a *cataplana-pan*, you may use instead a big stew-pan.

300g/11oz clams, cockles or mussels
(discard dead, opened ones)
150g/5½oz raw king prawns (see note about prawns on page 37)
4 small crayfish or small crabs
4 small squid
½ small garlic sausage, roughly sliced
2 onions, finely sliced
½ green pepper, seeded and sliced
½ red pepper, seeded and sliced
6 peeled tomatoes, finely chopped
4 garlic cloves, finely chopped
2 tbsp olive oil
1 tsp Piri-piri or Tabasco
1 bay leaf
1 tsp paprika powder
small bunch parsley
small bunch fresh coriander
1 glass white wine
Salt and pepper

1. Clean clams or mussels, put in a pan with 1 tbsp wine and heat until all the shells have opened. Shake pan occasionally.
Remove clams and discard empty shells and any others which haven't opened. Put the juice through a sieve or cloth and set aside.

Cleaning the squid

2. Clean squid well, removing ink from the inside of the body, removing the eyes and a beak-like bone in the middle of the tentacles (press it out). Rinse well and cut squid into slices.

3. Rinse and drain the prawns.
4. Remove legs and cut the crabs into halves.
5. Cover the bottom of the pan with onions and some garlic.
6. Pile up around the pan the seafood, squid, sausage, green and red peppers and tomato.
7. Sprinkle with paprika. Add bay leaf, parsley, coriander and leftover garlic.
8. Spoon olive oil, wine and juice all over the ingredients and season with salt and pepper.
9. Close the pan and simmer for about 20 minutes.

Serve straight from the pan. Saffron rice (see Side Dishes) could be served separately if you wish.

Prawns and squid on the spit

Cal. 470

Use wooden or metal skewers. For this dish you must use large raw tiger prawns complete with their heads and shells.

16 large raw prawns (see note about prawns on page 37)
4 squid gutted, washed and cut into slices (p. 35 nr.2)
100g/3½oz lightly smoked streaky bacon cut into small cubes
4 large tomatoes cut into wedges
2 green pepper, seeded and cut into large slices
2 onions cut into wedges
For the marinade
4 tbsp olive oil
4 garlic cloves, crushed
1 tsp paprika powder
1 tbsp Port wine
1 tsp Piri-piri
2 tsp mustard
Salt and pepper

1. Mix well together all the marinade ingredients. Add prawns and squid and set aside for about an hour.
2. Prepare skewers as following: first a piece of bacon, then a tomato wedge, a slice of pepper, an onion wedge, one prawn, a squid slice, bacon, tomato, pepper, onion etc.
3. Grill on low burning charcoal. Turn skewers around and brush occasionally with leftover marinade.
4. Garnish with lemon wedges. Serve immediately with a mixed salad (p. 41).
5. Provide a finger bowl with warm water and lemon slices.

Tip
Serve saffron rice timbales (see Side Dishes) with this dish.

Grilled king prawns
Cal. 160

King prawns and tiger prawns are the largest shrimps. They weigh about 30-40 g each. They come from Africa and South-eastern Asia and are frozen. Some expensive "fresh" ones are nothing but frozen ones, which have been thawed. If possible you should buy them fresh, complete with shell and head. If you are using frozen, defrost them slowly in the fridge, rather than in the microwave.
Note: *Wash, drain and cut them carefully along the back to remove the fine black digestive cord. Leave the heads on.*

600g/1½lb king prawns
5 tbsp vegetable oil
4 garlic cloves, crushed
2 tsp Piri-piri or Tabasco
1-2 tbsp sea salt
2 lemons, cut into wedges

1. Mix oil, garlic, Piri-piri and salt to make a sauce for basting.
2. Leaving heads on, cut prawns deep on the back and open them butterfly-like.
3. Brush prawns with the hot sauce.
4. Grill prawns on a <u>metal sheet</u> and continue to brush with sauce during cooking, until they are red on both sides. If grilled for too long they will become dry and fibrous.
5. Serve with lemon wedges and toasted bread, cut into triangles.
6. Provide a finger bowl with warm water and lemon slices.

Tip
If you are using a charcoal grill without a sheet metal, you may grill prawns on foil in which you have pierced some holes with a fork.

Clams Bulhão Pato

Cal. 250

Mr. Bulhão Pato was a romantic poet who lived in the XIX century in Lisbon. He loved clams and the Chef João da Mata invented this recipe for him. This dish is a classical served in good ale houses around the country.

1kg/2½lb clams (discard dead open ones)
1 tbsp butter or olive oil
1 onion, finely chopped
1 garlic clove, finely sliced
Small bunch fresh coriander
¼ glass vinegar
1 glass white wine
pepper
2 lemons, cut into wedges

1. Heat the butter or oil in a pan. Add onion and garlic and fry until softened.
2. Add clams, coriander, pepper, vinegar and wine.
3. Cover pan and cook without water until clams have opened. Discard the empty shells and any others which haven't opened.
4. Place the clams on a plate. Sieve the juice through a cloth over the clams.
5. Serve with lemon wedges and white bread.

Fish

Seafood or monkfish risotto
Cal. 480

500g/1¼ lb clams, cockles or mussels (discard dead, opened ones)
150g/5½ oz. raw king prawns (see note about prawns on page 37)

4 small crayfish or small crabs
4 small squid
or a 700g/1½ lb monkfish tail, skinned
2 tbsp olive oil
2 onions, finely sliced
2 garlic cloves, finely chopped
1 bay leaf
4 peeled tomatoes, finely chopped
Small bunch parsley, finely chopped
1 glass white wine
Piri-piri or Tabasco
300gr/11oz long grain or parboiled rice
Salt and pepper

1. **If you use seafood**, clean clams or mussels, put in a pan with 1 tbsp white wine and heat until all shells have opened. Discard the empty shells and any others which haven't opened. Strain the juice through a thin sieve or cloth and set aside.
2. Rinse and drain the prawns. Remove legs and cut the crabs into halves.
3. Clean squid well (see p. 35 nr.2)
4. **If you use monkfish**, wash the fish and cut the tail into pieces.
For both recipes:
5. Wash rice, bring to the boil in light salted water (2½ parts water for 1 part rice) and cook for 12 minutes. Strain the rice through a sieve and set aside.
6. Cover the bottom of a pan with all spices, white wine, tomatoes, parsley and sauce Piri-piri. Add some water, close pan and simmer for 30 minutes. If necessary add some water in the meantime.

Taste the sauce. Add a little bit of sugar If it is to bitter for your taste.

7. **Add all seafood**, except prawns, **or the monkfish** and enough water to cover ingredients. Let it cook about 15 minutes.

8. **If you use seafood add rice and prawns** and let it simmer until prawns turn red. **If you use monkfish add only rice** and let simmer for 3 minutes.

9. If necessary add a bit of water. Rice should remain moist.

10. Serve immediately.

Grilled sardines
Cal. 470

The best sardines are available after the month of June. Before summer they aren't fat enough to grill.

1.5kg/3¾lb or 16 sardines
Sea salt
1kg/2½lb potatoes
Bread
Charcoal grill or BBQ

1. Do not gut or remove scales from sardines if you intend to grill them. It is best not to rinse them either. The less they are handled the better.

2. Season each sardine well with sea salt and leave to stand for 30 minutes before grilling.

3. Grill sardines on both sides using a charcoal grill or barbecue. Be careful using a charcoal grill and take the necessary safety measures. Never use flammable liquids, such as petrol, as a firelighter! Charcoal needs to burn slowly. Keep a bottle of water handy and sprinkle the charcoal as soon as the flames start to get too high.

4. Serve with bread, boiled potatoes and a mixed salad.

Mixed salad with green peppers

½ lettuce, shredded
4 tomatoes cut into wedges
2 green peppers
1 onion, sliced
Sauce vinaigrette (see Sauces)

1. Grill peppers under a grill or in an oven until the skin bubbles. Then cool under cold water, peel off the skin and cut peppers into sticks.
2. Mix the salad ingredients together in a shallow bowl.
3. Season with vinaigrette sauce before serving.

Northern-style trout with bacon
Cal. 275

4 trout, each about 250g/9oz
4 rashers smoked streaky bacon
2 rashers smoked streaky bacon, chopped
4 tbsp butter
1 tbsp almonds, sliced
Plain flour
Salt
Lemon wedges to garnish

1. Season the fish with salt. Place one slice of bacon inside each fish.
2. Dust fish with flour and fry in butter, each side for 5-7 minutes. Set trout aside.
3. Add chopped bacon and almonds to butter and let it gently fry. Spoon it over trout and serve with boiled potatoes and lemon wedges.

Grilled "Loup de mer"

Cal. 345

4 "Loup de mer" each about 400g/14oz
3 tbsp olive oil
1 onion, finely chopped
Small bunch parsley, chopped
1 tsp paprika powder
1 tbsp oregano
sea salt and pepper

1. Let the fishmonger gut the fish for you. Mix onion and spices together and rub it well into the fish.
2. Wrap each fish loosely in aluminium foil.
3. Grill the fish for 10-15 minutes on a charcoal grill.
4. Serve with boiled potatoes and green vegetables.

Fisherman-style fish stew/Caldeirada

Cal. 645

The preparation of a "caldeirada" needs a certain skill, especially in the correct choice of fish and the trimming and gutting of it. Let the fishmonger help you if you're not experienced in its preparation. A first class fish stew, the way a fisherman would make, needs several sorts of fish, such as:
Conger eel - angel shark - sea bass or sea bream - red gurnard - sardines - ray - shrimps and clams.
*Use about 11 oz. of fish **per person** and choose larger fish rather than small ones.*

Serves 12

3.5kg/8¾lb assorted fish
500g/1¼lb clams
200g/7oz shrimps
3kg/7½lb potatoes, peeled and sliced
1kg/2½lb onions, sliced
1 big onion, sliced (it's the last ingredient)
2 green peppers, seeded and sliced

1kg/2½lb fresh tomatoes (or 2 large cans of peeled tomatoes), skinned and chopped
4 tbsp tomato purée
300ml/11 fl. oz. olive oil
3 garlic cloves, chopped
Sea salt and pepper
1 tsp Piri-piri or Tabasco
3 bay leaves
½ tbsp sweet paprika
1 tsp oregano
1 glass of white wine
1 small glass of Port wine
1 small glass of Whisky or Brandy
1 bunch parsley

For the soup:
100g/3½oz vermicelli
Mint sprigs, to serve

1. Use a large pan so the ingredients have plenty of room.
2. Heat 200ml/7fl.oz. of the olive oil and stir fry 2 tbsp tomato purée. Add the clams and make sure they are evenly distributed at the bottom of the pan (this helps prevent the other ingredients from burning). On top of the clams place the garlic, together with half of the parsley, onions, potatoes and green peppers.
3. Add the fish, the harder types, like conger and ray, should go underneath the softer ones like sea bass. Place the sardines on top.
4. Add the remaining onion, potatoes and green peppers.
5. Add tomatoes and shrimps. The last ingredient will be the big sliced onion and the remaining parsley.
6. Season with salt and pepper to taste. Add Piri-piri, bay leaves, paprika, oregano and all of the alcohol.
7. Ladle some olive oil over all ingredients and spices.
8. Cover the pan, bring to the boil and let it gently cook for 35 minutes. Shake the pan 1 or 2 times in the meantime.
9. Serve the caldeirada direct out of the pan into soup bowls.

Tips
1. You may shake the pan but <u>never</u> stir in it or the whole thing will turn into a mush.
2. Use a skimming ladle to serve, doing so without stirring.

Fish broth with vermicelli

After serving the caldeirada there remains a tasty broth. This can be eaten afterwards after the following:

1. Sieve the broth through muslin or a fine sieve.
2. Add some water to the sieved broth. Season with salt to taste, and then bring it to the boil.
3. Cook vermicelli in the broth and serve with some mint sprigs.

Fried small squid or cuttlefish
Cal. 380

*A **squid** is sea fish with tentacles at one end and a long, soft body. **Cuttlefish** looks like squid but has a round, hard body. They squirt out a black, inky liquid just as the octopus does.*

1kg/2½lb small squid or cuttlefish
Vegetable oil to fry
6 garlic cloves
1 bay leaf
100g/3½oz butter
1 small onion, finely chopped
1 tbsp chopped parsley
Juice of 1 lemon
Sea salt and pepper

1. Clean the squid (see p. 35, nr. 2). If you have used the cuttlefish, you must first remove the white shell inside the body. Small squid or cuttlefish do not need to be gutted.
2. Heat oil, season fish and fry it with bay leaf and garlic cloves. Remove garlic once it has changed colour. Do not allow it to burn.
3. Put squid aside and let it drain onto absorbent kitchen paper.
4. Melt butter in a pan. Add onions, parsley, lemon juice and pepper. Quickly stir fry onions soften without allowing them to cook too much. Season it with salt to taste.
5. Serve squid with saffron rice (see Side Dishes) and mixed salad. Serve the sauce separately.

Spicy squid curry

Cal. 460

You will find in Portuguese cookery there are some typical Indian dishes. Shrimp curry, chicken curry and fish curry are amongst the favourites.

1kg/2½lb medium sized squid
4 tbsp olive oil
1 onion, finely chopped
2 tbsp flour for dusting
1 apple, peeled and finely chopped
1 glass coconut milk (canned)
4 tomatoes, peeled and diced
½ tsp finely chopped fresh root ginger
2 tbsp curry powder or paste
Piri-piri or Sambal to taste
juice of ½ lemon
½ green pepper, finely chopped, to garnish
salt and pepper
250g/8oz Basmati or Thai jasmine rice

1. Use a wok or a stew-pan. Refer to cleaning of squid on page 35, nr.2. Cut squid into rings, leave tentacles whole if they are not too long. Season it with salt and pepper, dust with flour and steam in olive oil. Put squid aside.
2. Gently sweat the onion and spices in the same oil. Add lemon juice and apple and stir for a moment. Add coconut milk, then tomatoes and let it cook until sauce thickens slightly.
3. In the meantime cook the rice.
4. Add fried squid to the sauce and let cook it for 5 minutes. Season it to taste.
5. Sprinkle curry with chopped green pepper and serve with Basmati rice.

Roast mackerel fillet
Cal. 500

8 fresh, boneless firm mackerel fillets.

Tip
Buy four large mackerel. Use a pair of kitchen scissors to gut fish, remove scales and cut fins and gills off. Rinse and drain the fish. Ask the fishmonger to do it for you if you prefer. Cut the mackerel into halves, discard heads and remove bones.

1 leek, washed and cut into 1cm/0.4in slices
100ml/3½ fl. oz. olive oil
8 rashers lightly smoked streaky bacon
2 onions, sliced
2 tomatoes, sliced
1 tbsp paprika powder
Salt and pepper

1. Preheat the oven to 200°C/400°F. Season fillets with salt and pepper.
2. Heat one tbsp oil and stir fry the leek until softened. Remove leek and cover the bottom of a roasting pan with it. Place streaky bacon on the leek slices and then fillets on top. Sprinkle with paprika powder.
3. Cover fillets with onions and tomatoes. Pour over olive oil.
4. Roast for about 20 minutes.
5. Place fillets on a plate, spoon olive oil from pan over them and serve with homemade mashed potatoes (see Side Dishes).

Roast sea bream with garlic and olive oil

Cal. 590

1 sea bream or sea bass about 1.5kg/3¾lb
3 onions, sliced
5 garlic cloves, finely sliced
2dl/0.35pint olive oil
1 glass white wine
2 bay leaves
3 tomatoes, skinned, seeded and finely chopped
4 tsp paprika powder
Small bunch parsley
Sea salt and pepper
1kg/2½lb potatoes, peeled and coarsely diced

1. Preheat the oven to 200°C/400°F.
2. Ask the fishmonger to clean the fish for you. Put three small cross cuts on each side of the fish. Season with salt both inside and out. Place half of the garlic slices in the cuts and place the rest inside the fish, together with some parsley.
3. Cover the bottom of a roasting pan with 2/3 of the onions, add some olive oil and place the fish on top of the onions.
4. Spread tomato over the fish, sprinkle with 2 tsp paprika. Cover with the rest of the onions and parsley and place bay leaves on top. Spoon some olive oil over the whole fish and pour the white wine around it.
5. Bake for 30 - 40 minutes depending on how thick fish is.
6. In the meantime boil potatoes for ten minutes. Set aside in a bowl and mix with 2 tbsp olive oil and 2 tsp paprika.
7. Place potatoes around the fish 15 minutes before serving. Baste fish and potatoes occasionally with the sauce.
8. Serve fish slices from the roasting pan.

Swordfish steak with onions
Cal. 440

4 swordfish steaks each about 200g/7oz
4 onions, finely sliced
2 tbsp olive oil
2 garlic cloves, sliced
2 tbsp parsley, chopped
1 glass white wine
Juice of 1 lemon
3 tbsp margarine
Vegetable oil to fry
Salt and pepper

1. Prepare a marinade with the garlic, lemon juice, white wine, salt and pepper and marinade steaks for about 30 minutes. Reserve the marinade.
2. Heat vegetable oil and fry the steaks until they change colour on both sides. If they are fried for too long they will become dry and fibrous. Put aside and keep warm.
3. Heat olive oil. Add onions and marinade and allow cooking for 5 minutes.
4. Place each steak on a plate, spoon onions and sauce over.
5. Serve with boiled potatoes, sprinkled with chopped parsley.

Tuna steaks with tomato sauce

Cal. 500

4 tuna steaks each about 200g/7oz
Juice of 1 lemon
5 garlic cloves, sliced
1 bay leaf
Vegetable oil to fry

For the tomato sauce
1 tbsp olive oil
800g can of peeled tomato
1 tsp sugar
1 small onion, finely chopped
1 bay leaf
1 tsp oregano
1 tbsp celery, finely chopped
Salt and pepper

1. Prepare tomato sauce (see Sauces)
2. Season steaks with salt, pepper and lemon juice.
3. Heat vegetable oil. Add garlic and bay leaf, fry gently until they change colour then remove from pan and discard.
4. Fry tuna steaks until they change colour on both sides. If fried for too long they will turn dry and fibrous. Put aside and keep warm.
5. Heat tomato sauce. Add steaks and gently simmer for 2 minutes.
6. Serve with boiled potatoes sprinkled with parsley.

Fried fish and tomato rice
Cal. 370

1kg/2½lb mix of small fish such as mackerel, small slices of bigger fish such as sea bass, shrimps and squid
Flour to dust
Vegetable oil to fry
Black olives
2 lemons cut into wedges
Salt

1. Clean and salt the fish (p. 19, see Tips), then dust with flour.
2. Heat the oil and fry the fish until crispy on both sides. Let it drain on absorbent kitchen paper.
3. Serve with olives, lemon wedges and a mixed salad .

Tomato rice
Cal. 65

1 tbsp olive oil
1 small onion, chopped
1 garlic clove, chopped
1 bay leaf
2 large tomatoes, skinned, seeded and finely chopped
1 tbsp chopped parsley
250g/8oz long grain rice
Salt

1. Stir fry onion, garlic and bay leaf in oil until the onion has softened.
2. Add tomato and rice, mix together, add 1 liter/1¾ pint water.
3. Season with salt, bring to the boil and cook for 15 minutes. The rice should remain moist. Sprinkle with parsley and serve.

Roast eels with onions Franciscan-style

Cal. 675

800g/2lb eels, rinsed, drained cut into 2in pieces
Flour to dust
Vegetable oil to fry
2 onions, sliced
2 small bunches parsley, chopped
2 small bunches fresh coriander, chopped
1 lemon cut into wedges
Salt
For the sauce:
4 tbsp olive oil
3 tbsp vinegar
2 garlic cloves, crushed
Few strands saffron, lightly roasted in a dry pan, crushed and "dissolved" in some warm water
2 cloves
Pinch cumin
1 onion, finely chopped
1 tsp oregano
Salt and pepper

1. Season fish with salt and pepper, dust with flour.
2. Preheat the oven to 200°C/400°F.
3. Heat oil and fry fish quickly on both sides. Add onions, parsley and coriander on top, fry for another minute and set aside to drain on absorbent kitchen paper.
4. Place fish in a roasting pan.
5. Mix onions and all spices together in a bowl then spoon over the fish.
6. Bake until the sauce starts bubbling, no longer.
7. Garnish with lemon wedges.
8. Serve with mixed salad and small slices of white bread previously fried in vegetable oil.

Dried Salted Cod - Bacalhau

Portuguese get their bacalhau imported from Norway. Bacalhau takes a very important place in Portuguese cookery. A middle codfish weighs about 5lb. Ask the fishmonger to cut it into pieces of about 8x4in (20x10cm) or 150-200g/7oz each. Important: **Dried salted cod must be soaked overnight, thick cod up to two days and well rinsed.** *Thick cod must be soaked for up to two days. People say there are thousand ways of preparing salted cod. I have presented you with a few delicious ones, although cod is not to everyone's taste.*

Tips

Taste a piece of soaked row cod, so you can judge out how much salt you will need to cook it. Codfish need a lot of good olive oil to taste smooth.

Codfish with tomato sauce

Cal. 625

600g/1½lb salted cod, soaked overnight, well rinsed
 and cut into 3cm/1½in slices
3 tbsp flour
Vegetable oil to fry
500ml/17, 5 fl. oz. tomato sauce (see Sauces)
2 tbsp butter
1 tbsp parsley, chopped
Salt and pepper

1. Heat oil, dust cod with flour and fry for 5-10 minutes. Set aside and drain on absorbent kitchen paper.
2. Stir butter into tomato sauce. Season it to taste.
3. Place codfish on a plate. Spoon sauce over and sprinkle with parsley.
4. Serve with normal rice.

Codfish with vegetables and egg

Cal. 820

This is the way Portuguese eat cod on Christmas Eve. A medium cod weighs about 5lb. Let the fishmonger cut it into pieces of about 8x4in (20x10 cm) or 150-200g/7oz each.

4x200g/7oz salted cod, soaked overnight and well rinsed
1kg/2½lb potatoes, peeled and cut into halves
1kg/2½lb broccoli, trimmed and cut into small florets
4 whole carrots, peeled and cut into sticks
4 eggs
4 garlic cloves, finely chopped
1 bunch parsley, chopped
1 onion, finely chopped
For the dressing: olive oil, vinegar and pepper

1. Boil potatoes, carrots and eggs in salted water. Eggs should be hard boiled.
2. Boil broccoli florets until tender (3-4 minutes in boiling water).
3. Boil cod separately in lightly salted water for 15-20 minutes. Thick pieces of cod may need cooking a little longer.
4. Mix garlic with parsley and onion.
5. Serve cod, garnished with potatoes, carrot, egg halves and broccoli florets. Sprinkle with the garlic/onion/parsley mix.
6. Pour olive oil and vinegar over cod and vegetables and season with pepper to taste. Without the addition of **olive oil, vinegar and the onion/parsley mix** the whole dish will be a boring, dry meal!

Gomes de Sá's codfish (in the oven)

Cal. 625

Gomes de Sá was a wholesale fishmonger in Porto. This recipe was created for him by an unknown cook. Nowadays, every Portuguese is familiar with this dish.

600g/1½lb salted cod, soaked overnight, well rinsed and cut into four large pieces
500g/1¼lb boiled potatoes
250ml/8fl.oz. olive oil
100ml/3½fl.oz. milk
3 garlic cloves, finely sliced
2 onions, finely sliced
2 hard-boiled eggs, sliced
Bunch parsley, chopped
Black olives to garnish
Salt and pepper

1. Scald cod with hot water, keep it covered in a pan for 20 minutes then drain, remove skin and bone and break into small pieces.
2. Scald the pieces again with hot milk and cover for 2-3 hours.
3. Cut potatoes into large slices.
4. Preheat the oven to 180°C/350°F.
5. Heat olive oil in terracotta pot or any ovenproof casserole and fry onions and garlic until the onions are softened.
6. Add codfish and potatoes to the onions and bake for about 30 minutes or until potatoes are ready.
7. Garnish with hard-boiled egg, black olives, sprinkle with parsley and serve.

Codfish with Port wine

Cal. 500

600g/1½lb salted cod, soaked overnight, well rinsed and cut into four large pieces
500g/1¼lb clams (discard dead, opened ones)
1 glass white wine
small bunch parsley
1 bay leaf
500g/1¼lb skinned and peeled tomatoes, chopped
3 tbsp butter
1 onion, finely sliced
100ml/3½fl.oz. cream
100ml/3½fl.oz. Port wine
2 garlic cloves, finely sliced
2 cloves
1 tbsp flour
salt and pepper

1. Boil cod for 10 minutes, then drain, remove skin and bone then break into small pieces.
2. Place clams in a pan with wine, parsley and bay leaf. Heat it until all the shells are opened. Shake pan occasionally.
3. Remove clams from shells and discard empty shells and any others which haven't opened. Strain the juice through a sieve or cloth and set aside.
4. Melt 1 tbsp butter in a stew pan and cook tomato, onion, garlic and cloves for 5 minutes. Preheat the oven to 180°C/350°F.
5. Melt 2 tbsp butter in a sauce pan. Add flour and quickly stir until both are mixed. Add clam juice, Port wine, season with salt and pepper and simmer gently until sauce thickens slightly. Add cream, stir well without boiling and set aside.
6. Place cod in an ovenproof pan, cover with clams and tomato. Spoon over the sauce and bake until golden.
7. Serve with garlic rice (see Side Dishes).

Brás's codfish (with French fries)
Cal. 660

This dish is available in every good ale house. It is a delicious meal to eat with a glass of beer.

600g/1½lb salted cod, soaked overnight, well rinsed and cut into four large pieces
1kg/2½lb potatoes, cut into very thin chips each about 2-2½in long
2 onions, finely sliced
100 ml/3½fl.oz. olive oil
Vegetable oil to fry
3 eggs, beaten
Small bunch of parsley, finely chopped
200g/7oz black olives
salt and pepper

1. Boil cod for 10 minutes, then drain, skin and bone then mash with a fork until coarsely fibrous.
2. Fry potato chips lightly, season with salt and pepper and set aside.
3. Beat the eggs and add some parsley.
4. Heat olive oil in a stew pan. Stir fry onions until softened, add fried potato chips and cod. Cover the pan and simmer for a few minutes. Add egg and mix all ingredients together gently until the egg is cooked. The skill of this dish is to mix and cook the egg just until you get firm, but not rubbery, small egg pieces.
5. Place on a serving plate, sprinkle with parsley and season with freshly ground black pepper and garnish with black olives.

Tip
Instead of cooking the cod just mash it into small pieces and then stir fry gently with onions, potato and egg in olive oil.

Codfish my way (with cream)

Cal. 620

600g/1½lb salted cod, soaked overnight, well rinsed and cut into four large pieces
1 can sardines in olive oil
150ml/5fl.oz. olive oil
2 tbsp butter
1 onion, finely chopped
2 garlic cloves, finely sliced
Parsley, small bunch, chopped
1-2 tbsp flour
100g/3½oz Parmesan cheese or "Queijo da Ilha" from Azores
500ml/17½ pint milk
225ml/8fl. oz. cream
Salt and pepper
Pinch freshly ground nutmeg

1. Boil codfish for 10 minutes, then drain, skin and bone the cod and cut into small slices.
2. Drain and chop sardines. Heat 3 tbsp oil and butter, stir fry sardines with garlic and onions until onions have softened. Add parsley and remove from the heat.
3. Mix flour with half of the cheese. Dust codfish slices with it and set aside. Preheat oven to 180°C/350°F.
4. Spoon the olive oil into an ovenproof pan, place half of the cod slices in it and cover with half of the onion-sardine mix. Place the remaining cod on top and cover with remaining onions.
5. Stir milk into the cream, add a pinch of salt, pepper and nutmeg, and gently heat without boiling, then spoon over the cod.
6. Sprinkle with rest of the cheese and bake until golden.
7. Serve with mashed potatoes (see Side Dishes) or boiled sweet potatoes.

Poultry

Goa-style chicken curry
Cal.400

3 large boneless, skinless chicken breasts
4 tbsp olive oil
1 onion, finely chopped
2 tbsp flour for dusting
1 apple, peeled and finely chopped
1 glass coconut milk (canned)
4 tomatoes, peeled and chopped
½ tsp finely chopped fresh root ginger
2 tbsp curry powder or red curry paste if you like it hot
Piri-piri or chilli to taste
Juice of ½ lemon
4 slices pineapple, diced
½ green pepper, seeded and finely chopped
Salt and pepper
250 g/9oz Basmati or Thai jasmine rice

1. Use a wok or a stew-pan. Dice chicken breasts. Season with salt and pepper, dust with flour and stir fry in olive oil. Put chicken aside and keep warm.
2. Gently sweat the onion with all spices in some oil. Add lemon juice and apple and stir fry for a moment. Add coconut milk, then tomato and let it simmer until sauce thickens slightly.
3. In the meantime cook the rice.
4. Add fried chicken and pineapple to the sauce and let cook for 5 minutes. Season it to taste.
5. Sprinkle curry with chopped green pepper and serve with Basmati rice.

Monchique-style chicken

Cal.770

Monchique is the highest chain of mountains in the Algarve. This region is famous for:

*1. A very strong liquor called **Medronho**. The best Medronho is produced by farmers in illegal distilleries. You may taste it in the small taverns which are spread around the mountains if you ask for medronho caseiro.*
*2. A natural mineral water named **Água de Monchique**.*
*3. Some salted bacon **Presunto de Monchique**.*
*4. Dried fruits such as **figs**.*
*5. Delicious sausages such as **Farinheira** and **Morcela de carne**.*
*6. The chicken with the special wine sauce-**Frango à Monchique**.*

1.5kg/3 lb oven-ready chicken, cut into 8 pieces
(See Tip on next page)
2 tbsp flour
80g/2¾oz bacon (Monchique bacon or another), finely chopped
3 tbsp olive oil
1 onion, chopped
2 garlic cloves, crushed
800g/2lb peeled tomatoes (fresh or canned), finely chopped
1 tbsp sugar if using canned tomatoes
1 green pepper, seeded and finely sliced
½ of a small garlic sausage, sliced
1 tsp Piri-piri or hot chilli sauce
1 tsp paprika powder
Small bunch of parsley
1 bay leaf
½ bottle of white wine
Small glass Medronho liquor or Tequila
1½ glass Port wine
Salt

Tip
Cut technique to cut a chicken into eight pieces:

Holding the chicken breast firmly cut off the end joint of the drumsticks and the parsons' nose. Cut along one side of the breastbone from the body cavity to neck cavity. Spread open and cut along both sides of the backbone to remove it. Lay the chicken halves, skin side up, on a chopping board and cut diagonally between the breast and leg joints. Cut in half again to make eight pieces. Skin each of the pieces and discard skin. Season the chicken with salt and Piri-piri.

1. Place the flour in a polythene bag, then add the chicken pieces and shake to coat.
2. Heat oil in a casserole and fry bacon. Stir fry chicken pieces in melted fat until golden.
3. Add onion, garlic and tomato, green pepper, paprika, bay leaf, parsley and sausage and stir well.
4. Add white wine, Port wine and Medronho (or similar liquor), cover the casserole and cook for 30-45 minutes. Season it with salt to taste.
5. Serve with fried potatoes.

(Home) fried potatoes
Cal.180

600gr/1½lb potatoes boiled in salted water, roughly diced
Vegetable oil to fry
1 large onion, finely sliced
Salt and pepper

1. Heat oil and fry potatoes until golden.
2. Add onion and fry until softened.
3. Season with salt and pepper to taste.

Romeo's grilled chicken

Cal. 350

This is the grilled chicken which you can smell in the air at every folk festival and near thousands of "Churrasqueiras" around the country. The recipe for the paste I describe here was given to me by my old friend Romeo. He grilled his chicken in front of his Café in Odeceixe in the Algarve. He told me once that the real secret for his delicious "Frango" didn't lie just in the paste he used, but also on the fact that he never let his barbecue out of sight. He was right. Chicken burns very quickly. That's why you should always have a bottle of water near the barbecue to sprinkle on the fire when the flames get high.

2 oven-ready chickens, weighing about 1.5kg/3lb each
7fl.oz. vegetable oil
4 tbsp paprika paste
2 tbsp sea salt
Pepper and Piri-piri or chilli sauce to taste
6 garlic cloves, crushed
2 tsp paprika powder
2 tsp oregano

1. Cut chicken into halves.
2. Mix together all spices with a bit of oil. Rub chicken halves with half of this paste and allow marinating for about one hour. In the meantime light the barbecue and leave until charcoal burns slowly.
3. Mix remaining oil into remaining paste.
4. Grill the chicken on both sides and brush it several times with the mixture. Don't allow chicken to burn and grill it until both sides are golden and crispy.
5. Serve with French fries and mixed salad and serve some extra Piri-piri sauce separately.

Braga-style roast (wild) duck with rice
Cal. 980

2kg/5lb oven-ready duck
125g/4½oz Portuguese garlic sausage, finely sliced
125g/4½oz bacon, finely diced
2 onions, finely chopped
1 carrot, finely diced
2 oranges and 2 lemons, sliced
Juice of 2 oranges
1 glass vermouth
1 glass Port wine
250g/9oz long grain rice
30g/1oz hog's lard
50g/1¾oz butter
Salt and pepper

1. Use a large saucepan. Fill to the halfway mark with water, season with salt, add some orange and lemon slices to it and bring to the boil. Cook the duck gently in it for about one hour, then take aside to cool down and then cut it into eight pieces (see cut technique on p. 61). After skimming off the fat reserve the stock.
2. Preheat the oven to 200°C/400°F.
3. Place duck in an ovenproof pan, add half of the onion and the carrot. Brush duck with melted butter, season with pepper and put in the oven to roast. Occasionally turn pieces over to get them brown on all sides and pour some vermouth over them. As soon as all pieces are well browned pour orange juice and Port wine over and let it bubble for some minutes.
4. In the meantime stir fry left over onion in lard, add bacon, sausage and 500ml/17½ fl. oz. duck stock, bring to the boil, stir in rice and cook it for 10 minutes.
5. Put duck aside, pour in some water and stir well to incorporate any sediment from the bottom into the sauce. Stir the rice into the sauce and top with duck pieces. Cook in the oven until rice is tender and all the liquid has been absorbed.
6. Arrange on a serving plate and garnish with slices of orange and lemon.

Quails in Madeira sauce.

Cal. 395

4 quails, ready to cook
100g/3½oz butter
2 garlic cloves
½ glass white wine
½ glass Madeira wine
1 tsp gorse (wild herb) or rosemary
Salt and pepper

1. Rinse quails and pat dry with kitchen paper. Halve each quail lengthwise. Season it well with salt and pepper. Fry garlic cloves and gorse quickly in butter, then discard. Fry quail halves on both sides until browned.
2. Deglaze the pan with the white wine and then with the Madeira wine. Heat it until just bubbling, stirring and scraping the base and sides of the pan. Reduce until sauce thickens slightly.
3. Arrange quails on a serving plate. Pour sauce through a sieve over the quails. Serve with a vegetable purée (see Side Dishes).

Crispy turkey with stuffing
Cal. 800

4-5kg/10-12lb oven-ready turkey
For marinade:
2 oranges, sliced
2 lemons, sliced
200ml/7fl.oz. strong liquor such as Tequila or Grappa
1 tbsp salt
2 l/3½ pints water
For rubbing paste:
Mix well together
150g/5½oz hog's lard or margarine
100ml/3½fl.oz. olive oil
8 garlic cloves, minced
3 tbsp mustard
1 tsp fresh ground pepper
Juice of 1 lemon and
1 tbsp sea salt
For stuffing:
3 turkey livers, finely chopped
1 onion, finely chopped
50g/1¾oz butter
1 slice of white bread, crusts removed
2 beaten eggs
1 apple, peeled and finely chopped
50g/1¾oz bacon, chopped
3 tbsp chopped parsley
1 small glass Brandy
Salt and pepper
For sauce:
250ml dry white wine
1 small glass Brandy
1 tsp corn flour mixed into some water

1. Leave turkey in the marinade overnight. The following day pat dry with kitchen paper and rub well with the paste inside and out. Use rubber gloves to do it. Leave for about an hour.
2. Heat butter and stir fry onion and livers. Mix in crumbled bread, bacon, apple, parsley and egg. Add Brandy, season with salt and pepper to taste and knead the mixture.
3. Preheat oven to 200°C/400°F.
4. Fill turkey with stuffing (under breast skin as well) and sew cavities. Tie drumsticks together if desired. Bake in middle of oven for about 3 hours. Turkey must lie on its side. Turn it once. For the last 15 minutes turn it onto its back.
5. Cover turkey with foil and keep warm.
6. Deglaze the casserole with the wine, add Brandy and sieve the sauce.
7. Add corn flour and simmer until slightly thickened.
8. Serve with mashed potatoes and red cabbage.

Red cabbage with cumin

Cal. 25

½ head red cabbage, thinly sliced
4 bacon slices, chopped
1 onion, thinly sliced
1 tbsp hog's lard or margarine
1 bay leaf
1 tsp cumin seeds

1. Heat lard and stir in onion and bacon, fry until golden. Add cabbage, bay leaf, cumin and salt to taste. Cook, stirring occasionally until cabbage is very tender.

Tip
Serve as side dish with any kind of roasted meat or poultry.

Game

Hare or (wild) rabbit (quick way)
Cal. 430

500-700g/1¼-2lb hare or rabbit, cut into bite-sized pieces
3 tbsp olive oil
1 onion, finely chopped
150g/5½oz mushrooms
4 peeled tomatoes, seeded and halved
1 stick celery, thinly sliced
1 bay leaf
2 garlic cloves, crushed
1 sprig thyme
1 sprig fresh rosemary
1 bunch parsley
500ml/16fl.oz. white wine
Salt and pepper

1. Use a stew pan or a casserole. Season rabbit with salt and pepper and quickly stir in preheated olive oil.
2. Add vegetables, garlic and other spices. Pour in white wine and gently cook for about one hour or until rabbit is cooked through.
3. Discard herb sprigs and reduce sauce.
4. Serve with Portuguese fried cumin-potatoes (see Side Dishes) and fried bread triangles.

Fried bread triangles

Remove the crusts from eight slices of white bread and then cut them into triangles. Heat a little oil in a large frying pan and fry the triangles on both sides in batches until they are golden brown. Keep warm. Serve the rabbit on them.

The hunter's hare or (wild) rabbit

Cal. 430

Try to get well-hung venison if you like the gamey taste. Buy a fresh rabbit as frozen are sometimes extremely dry. Cut the hare or rabbit into eight pieces and let it coat in following marinade for 24 hours, using a terracotta pot (don't use a metallic pot).

1 bottle of red wine (1¼ pint)
6 garlic cloves, crushed
2 bay leaves
Salt and pepper
2 tbsp olive oil
1 tsp oregano

On the next day put aside and reserve marinade for cooking.
1 onion, finely chopped
1 tbsp chopped parsley
8 rashers lightly smoked streaky bacon
2 garlic cloves, minced
Salt and black pepper
3 glasses of marinade juice
1 tsp vinegar
Sprig gorse or 1 tsp ground gorse (wild herb) or
Sprig rosemary

1. Wrap each rabbit piece with a rasher of bacon. Tie each up with string and place in a casserole.
2. Add onion, parsley, garlic, pepper, gorse, marinade and vinegar. Cover and cook gently for one hour or until rabbit is cooked through. Season it with salt to taste. Remove lid from the casserole and reduce sauce.
3. Serve with Portuguese fried cumin-potatoes (see Side Dishes) and fried bread triangles (see foregoing page).

Stewed partridge with green peas purée
Cal. 450

Partridges should be hung for as long as possible before cooking. The season for partridge is from September to December. If a fresh partridge is unavailable, then they can be bought frozen from some grocers and supermarkets.

1 small partridge per person, well rinsed and patted dry
Enough rashers lightly smoked streaky bacon to wrap each of the partridges
12 shallots
4 small carrots, diced
2 tbsp butter
1 glass white wine
250ml/8fl.oz. chicken or game stock
Sprig of rosemary
Sprig of thyme
Salt and pepper

1. Season partridges inside and out with salt.
2. Wrap with rashers of bacon and tie.
3. Heat butter in a heavy casserole and stir fry shallots and carrots. Add partridges and brown on all sides. Pour in white wine, stock and some water. Add herb sprigs, season with salt to taste, cover and simmer very gently for about 2 hours, then discard herbs.
4. Serve each partridge on top of a green pea purée (see Side Dishes). Sieve the sauce and serve separately.
5. You may serve a delicious side dish alongside if you cook turnip slices together with partridges, 20 minutes before the end of cooking time. See also on page 28 the *Partridge consommé with turnips*.

Fried partridge with mushrooms

Cal. 355

4 boneless, skinless partridge breasts

To make use of bones and leftover parts of partridges, see recipe on page 28.

500g/1¼lb fresh mushrooms, such as chestnut and oyster, sliced
50g/1¾oz butter
1 tsp paprika powder
200ml/7fl.oz. cream
3 bunches parsley, chopped
100ml/3½oz chicken or game stock
Salt and pepper

1. Season partridge breasts with salt and pepper.
2. Heat some butter and gently fry breasts until golden. Put aside and keep warm.
3. Add some more butter to the pan. Sauté mushrooms until they begin to give off liquid. Season it lightly with salt and pepper. Add stock and simmer until slightly thickened. Add paprika and cream but do not allow boiling.
4. Arrange mushrooms on a plate, spoon sauce around and place partridge breasts on top. Sprinkle with parsley.

Tip
When fat "breaks up" through cream, add stirring a pinch water to homogenize it again.

Roasted pheasant with grapes
Cal. 500

1 ready-to-cook pheasant
4 rashers lightly smoked streaky bacon
1 glass red wine
150g/5½oz butter
1 tsp olive oil
100ml/3½fl.oz. chicken or game stock
2 tbsp Port wine
Salt and pepper
Mashed potatoes
250g/½lb grapes

1. Rinse pheasant well and pat dry with kitchen paper. Season it with salt and pepper. Wrap pheasant with bacon rashers and tie.
2. Preheat oven to 200°C/425°F.
3. Heat 2/3 of butter and oil in an ovenproof pan. Add pheasant and brown on all sides. Add some water and roast for 45 minutes, then remove bacon, discard and roast pheasant for 10 more minutes.
4. Prepare grapes and mashed potatoes while pheasant roasts. (see Side Dishes).
5. Take pheasant aside and keep warm. Deglaze pan with Port wine and stock, add remaining butter and simmer for 2 minutes.
6. Spoon sauce on a plate, place pheasant on it. Spoon the mashed potatoes on to a serving plate and serve grapes separately.

Meat

Plate of meat, vegetables and sausages
Cal. 530

This is the classic Portuguese dish nr.1 and it is a great favourite among Portuguese families. This rich meal is hard to digest. We never eat it at dinner but we can sit for hours "around" a cozido, with friends or family talking and eating till late in the afternoon.

Serves 6

500g/1¼lb rind less belly pork
500g/1¼lb piece of veal
1 chicken
1 smoked garlic sausage
1 smoked black sausage
(Portuguese morcela, Spanish morcilla)
1kg/2½lb potatoes
4 carrots, peeled and cut into large sticks
2 turnips, peeled and cut into wedges
1 head white cabbage, shredded
½ Savoy cabbage, shredded
200g/7oz brown beans
200g/7oz rice
Salt

1. Use a pressure cooker. Bring salted water to the boil. Cook meat, sausages and beans for 15 minutes. Put meat and sausage aside, sieve beans from broth, reserve broth.
2. Cook all vegetables in broth until tender.
3. Put about ¾ pint broth aside and cook the rice in this for 15 minutes.
4. Return the meat and sausages to the vegetable broth.
5. Cut meat and sausages into slices. Serve in the middle of a large plate, vegetables around the edge. Ladle hot broth over and serve beans separately.

Red bean stew

Cal. 540

Before discovering South America the Portuguese cooked this dish using lentils. The basic ingredients for a bean stew are dried, smoked and salted products. They were common food on Portuguese sailing ships by the time of the discoveries and so it arrived. **Feijoada** *is now a classical Brazilian dish but the original recipe belongs to the North-eastern Portuguese province of Trás-os-Montes.*

500g/1¼lb brown or black beans (or lentils) soaked overnight
500g/1¼lb pork, cut into cubes
(Brazilian use dried meat)
1 garlic or paprika sausage, sliced
1 black sausage *(morcela)*, sliced
1 salted hog's ear*, well-scrubbed and trimmed
500g/1¼lb smoked streaky bacon, chopped
1 salted pig's trotter*, well-scrubbed and cut in half
1 large onion, diced
3 carrots, finely sliced
2 garlic cloves
3 tbsp olive oil
800g (can) peeled tomato, finely chopped
Pinch sage
1 tsp cumin
1 glass white wine
200g/7oz long grain rice
For the Brazilian way
2 oranges, sliced
2 tbsp butter
100g/3½oz manioc flour

*A lot of Portuguese like pig's trotters and hog's ears. If you're not used to eating them, substitute with more sausage (garlic sausage/*chorizo*, black pudding/*morcela*) or pork.

1. Use a pressure cooker and cook meat and beans for 15 minutes in unsalted water.
2. In a large pan heat the olive oil. Fry onion, carrots and garlic gently for 5 minutes until softened and lightly browned.
3. Add white wine, tomato and cumin. Reheat whilst stirring and cook slowly for 15 minutes.
4. Add meat and sausages. Add some broth until the beans are just covered. Season it with salt to taste and cook slowly for another 15 minutes.
5. Cook rice in broth (1 part rice to 2 of broth) until broth is absorbed.
6. Stir fry manioc flour in melted butter to *farina;* it gets a bit roasted and gives a fine aroma.
7. Serve feijoada with a rice timbale, a spoon of *farofa* and garnish with slices of orange.

Roast leg of pork
Cal. 490

2kg/5lb leg of pork, skin scored into diamonds
1 tsp paprika powder
4 garlic cloves, minced
1 tsp marjoram or rosemary
1 tbsp olive oil
Salt and pepper
250ml/8 fl. oz. white wine or beer
For the sauce
1 tbsp olive oil
1 garlic clove
1 cup pork stock, reserved after cooking leg
2 egg yolks
Juice of 1 lemon

1. Bring lightly salted water to the boil. Boil leg of pork quickly (5-10 minutes).
2. While pork cooks, mix salt and spices with olive oil.
3. Remove leg, pat dry, let it cool down so that you can handle it and rub it with the spice mix.
4. Preheat the oven to 180°C/350°F.
5. Place leg in a roasting tin, then place in the oven and roast for about 2-2½ hours (see Tip). 30 minutes before the end of cooking time pour over white wine or beer.
6. Put leg aside, wrap in foil and keep warm.
7. Deglaze roasting tin with pork stock and strain the sauce.
8. Stir fry lightly a whole garlic clove in olive oil, then discard clove. Then add the olive oil to pork sauce. Bring to the boil, then remove from heat and stir egg yolks in until the sauce thickens. Add lemon juice to taste and season well with pepper.
9. Serve with roast potatoes and roast apples.

Tip
1. Calculate 30 minutes cooking time per 450g/1lb pork.

Stewed veal with wine
Cal. 540

750g/2lb lean veal, chopped thickly
125g/4½oz smoked bacon, chopped
6 garlic cloves
1 bay leaf
½ bottle red wine (Bordeaux like)
2 tbsp olive oil or margarine
2 onions, roughly chopped
400g/1lb carrots, finely diced
1 tsp oregano
2 tbsp plain flour
1 small glass Brandy
1 tsp marjoram
Salt and pepper

1. Prepare a marinade with wine, garlic, bay leaf, salt and pepper and let the meat marinade for 3-4 hours.
2. Heat oil or margarine in a heavy casserole and stir fry veal and bacon until brown. Pour over Brandy. Add onion and carrot and dust with flour whilst stirring. Add marinade a little at a time scraping the bottom of the pan. Add water, if necessary, to cover ingredients.
3. Bring to the boil and then simmer gently for 1-1½ hour or until meat is cooked through. 20 minutes before end of cooking time add marjoram and oregano and cook uncovered until the sauce thickens slightly.
4. Serve veal with pasta such as *penne* or *rigatoni,* cooked *al dente** and sieve sauce before you spoon it over.
* **Al dente** = cooked just enough to be still firm when bitten.

Noodles with pork

Cal. 450

This is the only pasta dish we consider as Portuguese. Otherwise almost no noodles are used as main dishes in our cookery.

500g/1¾ lb lean pork, cut into 1-inch cubes
½ smoked Portuguese garlic sausage, sliced
1 onion, roughly chopped
1 tbsp olive oil
1 tbsp butter
2 garlic cloves, crushed
400g peeled tomatoes, chopped
1 tsp sugar
½ glass white wine
Salt and pepper
300g/11oz noodles
4 leaves of lettuce, rolled and thinly sliced

1. Use a pressure cooker if possible for this recipe. Heat the olive oil and the butter. Stir fry pork.
2. Add onion, garlic, sausage, tomato, wine and sugar. Season it with salt to taste.
3. Fill with enough water to just cover pork, close pressure cooker and cook for about 15-20 minutes, (40 minutes in an ordinary pan).
4. Open cooker, add 2 cups of water, correct seasoning, bring to the boil and cook noodles (in open cooker) *al dente** for about 7-8 minutes. The sauce must thicken a little. So allow to stand for 5 minutes.
5. Place noodles and pork in a shallow bowl and mix in the lettuce. Season with freshly ground pepper and serve immediately.

* **Al dente**=cooked just enough to be still firm when bitten.

Beira-Alta-style pot-roasted goat or mutton
Cal. 500

If you dislike the taste you need to trim, so far as possible, every piece of fat, tendons and especially the tallow glands. Perhaps the butcher can do it for you.

1.5kg/3½lb goat or mutton (neck or saddle)
2 tbsp olive oil
2 tbsp hog's lard
3 onions, finely sliced
2 garlic cloves, crushed
1 tsp paprika powder
2 bay leaves
½ tsp clove powder
1 bunch parsley
1 bottle red wine
Salt and pepper
700g/1½lb potatoes

1. Preheat the oven to 145°C/300°F.
2. Trim meat of fat and cut meat into large individual portions.
3. Prepare a marinade with red wine, garlic, bay leaves, paprika powder, salt and pepper and marinade meat pieces for 8 hours.
4. Place ½ of the onion on the bottom of a terracotta casserole. Lay meat pieces on it. Cover meat with rest of onions. Pour olive oil over. Season it with clove powder. Add lard and parsley and fill with the marinade until meat is covered.
5. Cover with a lid or foil and braise in the oven for 2 hours.
6. Boil potatoes in salted water while meat braises and cut into large wedges. Add potatoes to the meat 20 minutes before end of cooking time.
7. Vegetable purées taste wonderful with it (see Side Dishes).

Pork loin with clams

Cal. 620

Carne de porco à alentejana. *This dish is the highest point on combining seafood with pork meat. Originally created in the Southern province Alentejo, it is so delicious that it is now available all over the country and almost seen as one of our national delicacies. The Portuguese disagree about if this dish should be prepared or not with potatoes. I first prepare this dish without potatoes and add pre-boiled potatoes later on, so that they mop up the sauce.*

1kg/2½lb lean pork, roughly diced
1 bottle white wine
1kg/2½lb clams, well rinsed (discard dead, opened ones)
4 garlic cloves, crushed
1 tbsp paprika paste
50g/1¾oz hog's lard or margarine
1 tbsp olive oil
2 onions, chopped
½ green pepper, finely chopped
½ tsp Piri-piri or chilli sauce
200g can peel tomatoes, chopped
2 bay leaves
1 tsp paprika powder
1 bunch fresh coriander
Salt and pepper
2 lemons cut into wedges
200g/7oz black olives
700g/1½lb potatoes, roughly diced, cooked in boiling, salted water for 15-20 minutes

1. Marinade pork for 3-4 hours in a marinade made of white wine, 3 crushed garlic cloves, bay leaves, paprika and pepper. Then remove and discard garlic and bay leaves.

2. Pat pork dry and coat in paprika paste, season with salt and stir fry in hot lard until browned.
3. Deglaze pan with half of the marinade and reduce sauce. Put aside.
4. Put clams in a pan with ¼ of the marinade wine and heat until all the shells have opened.
5. Shake pan occasionally. Remove clams and discard empty shells and any others which haven't opened. Strain the juice through a sieve or cloth and set aside.
6. Heat oil in a pan. Prepare a roux stirring onion and garlic in hot olive oil. Add green pepper and tomato and simmer for a while.
7. Add clams and clam juice, pork and pork sauce and mix gently.
8. 5 minutes before serving add boiled potatoes to the pan, and bring to the boil for a minute.
9. Serve on a plate and garnish with black olives and lemon wedges. Sprinkle with fresh chopped coriander.

Kid or Lamb stew with vegetables

Cal. 580

1.5kg/3½lb trimmed kid or lamb (neck or saddle)
3 tbsp olive oil
3 onions, finely chopped
3 garlic cloves, crushed
200g fresh green peas or green beans
1kg/2½lb potatoes
4 carrots, peeled and roughly diced
1 green pepper, seeded and sliced
1 turnip, peeled and sliced
500ml white wine
1 small glass Brandy
½ tsp cumin seeds
1 bay leaf
Salt and pepper

1. Cut meat into large individual portions.
2. Heat olive oil and stir fry meat until browned. Season it with salt and pepper. Add garlic and onion. Pour Brandy and simmer for about 2 minutes.
3. Fill with wine and some water until meat is covered. Bring to the boil and cook for about 40 minutes.
4. Peel potatoes and cut into eighths.
5. Peel green peas (using fresh ones) or drain canned peas.
6. Add all vegetables, cumin and bay leaf to meat 20 minutes before end of cooking time. Season it with salt to taste.
7. After cooking time let stew stand for 15 minutes before serving.

Testing goat and mutton meat cooking times - different kinds of this meat may have different cooking times. Test if meat is cooked through Halfway through the cooking time. Too long cooking and meat will "dissolve" in the sauce.

Fried Pork loin cubes
Cal. 320

2kg/5lb pork steak, roughly diced
5 garlic cloves, minced
1 tbsp oregano
1 tbsp vinegar
1 tea cup olive oil
1 tbsp paprika paste
6 bay leaves
500g/1¼lb hog's lard
Fresh ground pepper

Accompaniment:
Potatoes
Lemon wedges
Mixed pickles
Black olives

1. Stir together garlic, oregano, vinegar, olive oil, fresh ground pepper and paprika paste in a large bowl. Coat pork cubes with it.
2. Place them in a <u>terracotta</u> pot. Keep pot for 2-3 days in a cool dry place and turn pork occasionally during that time to coat.
3. Heat some lard and sauté rojões until they change colour. As soon as the colour changes take rojões out and place in a dry clean <u>terracotta</u> pot together with bay leaves.
4. Melt remaining lard and fill pot up until all the meat is covered with fat. Let it cool down, cover pot air-tight with a cling film and keep in a cool dry place. You can preserve rojões this way for some weeks.
5. Whenever you need "rojões", take them out with a spoon, ready-sautéed in their own fat and season with salt.
6. Serve with home-fried potatoes (p. 61), lemon wedges, mixed pickles and black olives.

Lisbon-style liver thin cutlet

Cal 483

Tips
1. Freeze the liver lightly and cut into very thin slices using a slicing machine if possible.
2. If possible, use hog's lard for frying.

750g/2lb calf or pigs liver slices
2 onions, sliced
2 tbsp plain flour
4 garlic cloves, finely sliced
1 glass vinegar
1 glass white wine
1 bay leaf
2 tbsp ketchup or 1 tbsp tomato purée
Salt and pepper
3 tbsp hog's lard
1kg/2½lb potatoes, sliced
1 tbsp parsley, finely chopped

1. Prepare a marinade using the vinegar, garlic, salt and pepper, bay leaf and ketchup. Marinate the liver overnight and then discard the marinade.
2. Heat hog's lard and fry liver on both sides. Put aside and keep warm.
3. Coat onion with flour and stir fry in same fat. Place fried onion on liver.
4. Deglaze the pan with white wine. Season it to taste. Sieve the sauce to remove the lumps.
5. Serve with boiled potatoes and sauce. Sprinkle with parsley.

Steaks – Bifes

The Portuguese loves"bifes" (from the English „beef"). If a Portuguese isn't too sure what to order, he will order a steak with French fries -"um bife com batatas fritas" or - the same but with a fried egg on top of it "um bife com um ovo a cavalo". In Portugal steak replaces the hamburger. Children are used to the "bitoque" which is a small steak, French fries, an egg and a lot of sauce to soak their bread in. For about 7 € or 5 £ it is the ultimate competitor to his minced relative. A steak needs to be about 180g/6oz in weight, about 1 inch thick, and a very good flat piece of beef (like sirloin). Beside the quality of the meat, the success of a steak lies in the delicious sauces and on the cooking times:

Rare: *sauté or grill 2 minutes on each side.*
Medium rare: *sauté or grill 4 minutes on each side.*
Well done: *sauté or grill 5-6 minutes on each side.*
(The times given are for a 1 inch thick piece of beef).

Tips
1. Never use a steak which has just come from the fridge. First let it stand until it reaches room temperature, otherwise it may become tough by frying.
2. Never hammer a steak. Good quality meat doesn't need it.
3. Season steaks before cooking - brush with oil but do not salt, until they have been turned once.
4. Begin with a high heat and then reduce to the half heat. If you intend to fry a medium rare steak, first fry each side 2 minutes on high heat, then 2 minutes on medium heat.
5. Turn steaks without piercing them - do not use a fork to turn them - otherwise they will lose their juices and become dry and tough.

Portuguese-style veal steak

Cal. 550

4 veal steaks each about 180g/6oz
5 garlic cloves, minced
1 tbsp vinegar
4 rashers smoked bacon
3 tbsp olive oil
150g/5½oz butter
1 bay leaf
1 tsp lemon juice
½ tea cup Brandy
1 lemon, cut into wedges
4 eggs
Mixed pickles
Salt and fresh ground black pepper

1. Stir together 4 minced garlic cloves, vinegar, 1 tbsp olive oil and fresh ground black pepper in a shallow dish.
2. Brush steaks with this marinade.
3. Heat remaining olive oil and stir fry 1 garlic clove and bay leaf for 1 minute then discard.
4. Sauté steaks for 1 minute on each side. Season with salt; reduce the heat and sauté for another 2-4 minutes on each side. Transfer to plates and keep warm.
5. Fry bacon a little in the same fat and top each steak with one rasher of fried bacon.
6. Discard half of the fat. Deglaze pan with brandy, let it simmer for a moment and add the butter. Spoon the sauce over the steaks.
7. Serve with **French fries**, **fried egg** and garnish with **mixed pickles** and **esparregado** (see Side Dishes).

Tip: Fry eggs in butter, without seasoning.

Escalope of veal with Madeira wine sauce

Cal. 550

8 thin pieces of veal each about 100g/3½oz
Plain flour to dust
100g/3½oz butter
4 tbsp demi-glace ready-made sauce
1 small bunch parsley, finely chopped
250ml/9fl.oz. Madeira or Port wine
Salt and pepper

1. Dust veal with flour. Heat butter and fry escalopes 3 minutes on each side. Season them with salt and pepper when turning. Transfer to plates.
2. Add demi-glace sauce to deglaze pan and let simmer for a while. Pour in Madeira wine, sprinkle with parsley and reduce. Adjust seasoning.
3. Spoon sauce over escalopes and serve with carrot purée (see Side Dishes) and flat pasta such as tagliatelle.

Portuguese small pork cutlets/Bifanas

Cal. 80-95 each cutlet

These are the original "Bifanas", which Portuguese usually eat in rolls with mustard. You may order also Bifanas on a plate which are served with French fries and mixed pickles. They can lay be eaten as a snack whenever you are hungry.

2kg/4½lb pork steak in one piece
5 garlic cloves, minced
1 tbsp oregano
1 tbsp vinegar
1 tea cup olive oil
1 tbsp paprika paste
6 bay leaves
500g/1¼lb hog's lard
Fresh ground pepper

1. Freeze pork lightly and cut into 5mm/0.2in thin cutlets using a sharp knife.
2. Stir together the garlic, oregano, vinegar, olive oil, fresh ground pepper and paprika paste in a large bowl. Coat pork slices with it.
3. Pile them up in a *terracotta* pot. Keep pot for 2-3 days in a cool dry place and turn cutlets once in a while during that time.
4. Heat some lard and sauté Bifanas just until they change colour. As soon as the colour changes take the cutlets out and pile them up in a dry clean *terracotta* pot with bay leaves between them.
5. Melt remaining lard and fill pot up until all the meat is covered with fat. Let it cool down, cover pot air-tight with cling film and keep in a cool dry place. You can preserve cutlets this way for some weeks.
6. Whenever you need Bifanas, take them out with a spoon, ready-sautéed in their own fat and season with salt. If you wish prepare with your favourite sauce, adding some wine or cream.

Side Dishes

Green cabbage purée/Esparregado
Cal. 175

You can prepare this dish with any type of green cabbage.

1kg/2½lb green leaves
3 tbsp olive oil
1 garlic clove, crushed
1 bay leaf
1 tbsp flour
1 tsp vinegar
Salt and pepper

1. Cook leaves in salted water until tender, then chop finely. Reserve the cooking water.
2. Heat oil. Fry garlic and bay leaf. Remove bay leaf, then add green leaves and fry for 2 minutes.
3. Whisk flour with a cup of cooking water, pour onto vegetables and cook until the whole thickens.
4. Season with vinegar and pepper to taste.

Green pea purée

1kg/2½lb fresh green peas or an 800g can
1 tsp sugar
1 tbsp cream
Pinch nutmeg

1. Drain green peas. Cook or heat them in salted water with sugar and freshly ground nutmeg.
2. Purée green peas in a food processor or blender, or by pushing through a sieve.
3. Add cream, stirring until smooth.
4. Season to taste with pepper.

Carrot purée

8 coarsely grated carrots
1 tbsp cream

1. Cook grated carrot in salted water, drain and purée.
2. Whisk cream and carrot purée until smooth.

Mashed potatoes

Cal. 135

1kg/2½lb potatoes
200ml/7fl. oz. warm cream or milk
1 tbsp butter
Pinch nutmeg
Salt and pepper

1. Peel potatoes, cook in salted water for 20 minutes, then drain.
2. While still hot, mash potatoes well with a fork.
3. Warm milk or cream and ground nutmeg, pepper and butter.
4. Stir spiced milk into potatoes. Season it with salt, nutmeg and pepper to taste.

Garlic rice

Cal. 45

Rule for rice: 1 part of rice to 2 of water
1 tbsp olive oil
½ onion, finely chopped
2 garlic cloves, minced
1 bay leaf
150g/5½oz long grain rice
500ml/¾ pint water

1. Heat oil. Make a roux with onion, garlic and bay leaf.
2. Add rice and fry gently. Add water, season with salt and pepper and cook for 15-20 minutes. Discard bay leaf, stir with a fork and serve.

Saffron rice
Cal. 45

Rule for rice: 1 part of rice to 2 of water
1 tbsp olive oil
½ onion, finely chopped
150g/5½oz long grain rice
500ml/¾ pint water
Few strands saffron
Salt

1. Heat oil. Fry onion, add water and season with salt. Bring to the boil.
2. Add rice and cook for10 minutes.
3. Roast saffron lightly in a pan, then dissolve with 1 tbsp of warm water and add to the rice. Cook for another 8 minutes until tender. Stir rice with a fork and serve.

Grapes in Port wine syrup
Cal. 115

400g/1lb grapes
4 tsp sugar
2 tbsp Port wine
50g/1¾oz butter

1. Peel and de-seed grapes.
2. Heat sugar in a pan with 3 tbsp water until it became a syrup.
3. Add grapes and Port wine.
4. Add small pieces of butter one at the time, swirling the pan until the syrup thickens slightly.
5. Remove grapes carefully with a skimming ladle and serve.

Fried potatoes with cumin

Cal. 180

600gr/1½lb potatoes, peeled and cubed, cooked and drained.
Vegetable oil to fry
2 tsp cumin seeds
Salt and pepper

1. Fry potatoes until golden. Sprinkle with cumin seeds. Season it with salt and pepper to taste.

Sweets and convent desserts

Most Portuguese desserts have their origins either in Moorish culture or in Christian convents from the middle ages.

Attention: No calories counts for sweets. It is a subjective risk.

Cherubim's pudding

250g/9oz sugar
8 egg yolks
4 egg whites
1 cinnamon stick
½ tsp ground cinnamon

1. Cook sugar with cinnamon stick in a small non-stick pan, swirling the pan, until you have a melted and golden caramel (normally it will take 9-10 minutes over moderately low heat). Remove from heat and allow cooling. Discard cinnamon stick.
2. Beat egg yolks with an electric whisk until smooth. Add to caramel and cook stirring until you can see bottom of pan. Remove again from the heat.
3. Whisk the egg whites and then fold into the yolk mixture.
4. Transfer to a plate and sprinkle with ground cinnamon.

Angel's cheeks – Papos-de-anjo

Serves 12

8 egg yolks (2 for 3 portions)
20g/¾ oz. butter
12 custard cups or ramekins

1. Preheat oven to 145°C/300°F.
2. Beat egg yolks with an electric whisk until smooth.
3. Brush cups with melted butter.

4. Divide egg yolk among greased cups, filling halfway and bake in a water bath (Bain Marie) for about 10 minutes or until ready.
5. Remove cups from water bath and cool on a rack. De-mould by inverting onto plates.

For the sugar syrup
500g/1¼lb sugar
1 cinnamon stick
250ml/9fl.oz water
1 small glass of Port wine
Rind of a no-waxed lemon

1. Simmer water, sugar, lemon rind and cinnamon until melted and pale like golden syrup (normally this will take 6 minutes over moderately low heat).
2. Add Port wine stirring and discard lemon and cinnamon stick. Let syrup cool down and transfer Angel's cheeks to the syrup to coat.
3. Serve chilled.

"Heaven's streaky bacon"/Toucinho do céu

500g/1¼lb sugar
250g/9oz finely ground almonds
12 egg yolks
2 egg whites
2 tbsp butter
2 tbsp all-purpose flour
1 tsp ground cinnamon
Caster sugar to dust

1. Preheat the oven to 200°C/400°F.
2. Grease and flour an 18cm/7in cake tin.
3. Whisk egg yolks until smooth.
4. Whisk egg whites with flour until stiff.
5. Cook sugar in 250ml/9fl.oz. water until it thickens to a syrup. Add almonds and simmer, stirring for some minutes.

6. Add egg yolk, egg white, butter and cinnamon. Stir well and simmer, until mixture thickens slightly. Turn into the prepared tin and bake until a fine skewer inserted in the cake comes out clean.
7. Cool in the tin for 15 minutes; turn out on to a wire rack or plate and cool completely. Dust with caster sugar.

Threads of egg yolk in sugar syrup

500g/1¼lb sugar
12 egg yolks
2 egg whites
Cinnamon

1. Whisk egg yolks and whites until smooth.
2. Cook sugar in 250ml/9fl.oz. water until it thickens to a syrup.
3. Pour egg spiral-wise from the edge to the middle of syrup, using a very thin funnel. Stop stirring and cook until thickened.
4. Remove from heat, spoon onto a saucer, sprinkle with cinnamon and serve cold.

Milk pudding

500ml/¾ pint milk
1 tbsp flour
200g/7oz sugar
4 egg yolks
1 tsp finely grated rind of 1 no-waxed lemon

1. Whisk milk with flour. Add sugar, bring slightly to the boil and let it cool down.
2. Fold egg yolk and lemon rind into the mixture; bring slightly to the boil (moderate heat).
3. Spoon onto saucers and sprinkle with sugar.
4. Burn sugar by placing under a very hot grill.
5. Serve chilled.

Father Antonio's dessert

½ a loaf of toast bread, thickly sliced
50g/1¾oz butter
500ml/17½ fl. oz. white wine
4 tbsp honey
1 tsp cinnamon
Rind of 1 no-waxed lemon

1. Preheat the oven to 200°C/400°F.
2. Cut slices of bread into 2,5 cm/1 inch sticks.
3. Toast bread sticks, brush with butter and arrange in a 33x23cm/13x9in Swiss roll tin.
4. Simmer stirring in white wine, honey, cinnamon and lemon until it becomes syrup.
5. Cool syrup down and pour over bread sticks.
6. Bake until syrup reduces to 1/3 of its volume.
7. Serve warm.

Special Christmas fritters

These fritters are a traditional Christmas dessert. You can prepare them without the special sauce and you may substitute red wine for milk. All varieties taste delicious.

½ a loaf of toast bread, thickly sliced
¾ pint milk
3 eggs, beaten
1 tbsp sugar
½ tbsp ground cinnamon
Pinch salt
100g/3½oz butter to fry

1. Coat slices one at a time in milk, then in lightly salted beaten egg and fry in butter until golden.
2. Mix sugar with cinnamon. Sprinkle fried slices with it if you are serving them without sauce.

For the sauce:
6 dried figs, roughly chopped
1 tbsp pine nuts, roughly chopped
2 tbsp honey
10 shelled walnuts, roughly chopped
1 tbsp raisins or sultanas
2 glasses of Port wine
3/4 pint water

1. Cook nuts and honey in water and Port wine for ¾ hour.
2. Spoon over fried bread slices and sprinkle it with sugar-cinnamon mixture.

Golden Soup

500g/1¼lb sugar
100g/3½oz brown bread, without crust and diced
2 tbsp butter
100g/3½oz finely ground almonds
10 egg yolks, whisked
1 tsp ground cinnamon

1. Cook sugar in 250ml/9fl.oz. water until it thickens to a syrup (9-10 minutes).
2. Heat butter and fry bread, then coat with the syrup.
3. Add almonds and egg yolk stirring and cook until stiff.
4. Remove from heat, place onto a plate, make into a circle, sprinkle with cinnamon and serve cold.

Siricaia or Sericá

"Sericaia" is a very old sweet which originates from Elvas, a town on the border of Spain. I know two recipes for this sweet.

Recipe nr.1
6 egg yolks
150g/5¼oz sugar
250ml/9fl. oz. milk
1 tsp grated rind of a no-waxed orange

1. Preheat the oven to 200°C/400°F.
2. Whisk egg yolks with sugar until smooth.
3. Bring milk and orange rind gently to the boil.
4. Add egg yolks stirring and remove from heat.
5. Divide egg yolk among greased cups and bake in a water bath (Bain Marie).

Recipe nr. 2
500ml/17½fl. oz. milk
4 tbsp flour
250g/9oz sugar
1 tsp grated rind of a no-waxed lemon
7 egg yolks
7 egg whites, whisked until stiff

1. Preheat the oven to 250°C/500°F.
2. Whisk flour into the milk. Add sugar and lemon and bring gently to the boil. Remove from heat.
3. Fold egg yolk then egg white into the milk. Mix well and divide mixture among greased cups. Bake in a water bath (Bain Marie).

Sweet milk-rice

750ml/1¼ pint milk
250g/9oz round grain rice
250g/9oz sugar
3 egg yolks, beaten
1 vanilla pod, split lengthwise
Pinch salt
Ground cinnamon to decorate.

1. Rinse rice in water and drain.
2. Cook the rice for 10 minutes in milk with vanilla pods and a pinch of salt over moderate heat. Add sugar and cook for another 5 minutes, then discard vanilla pods.
3. 5 minutes before end of cooking time set some rice aside and fold egg yolk into it. Add this rice to the other and cook until ready.
4. Spoon into dishes and allow cooling. Decorate with cinnamon.

Pumpkin éclairs

1.2kg/2¾lb pumpkin squash or wedge, seeded, peeled and diced
1 egg yolk
1 tsp grated rind of a no waxed orange
100g/3½oz flour
1 tsp baking powder
2 tbsp sugar mixed with 1 tbsp cinnamon
Vegetable oil to fry

1. Cook pumpkin, drain and purée. Stir in egg yolk and orange rind.
2. Sift together the flour and baking powder and then fold into pumpkin purée.
3. Heat oil in a deep frying pan, form small portions of purée with 2 spoons and fry on both sides. Drain on kitchen paper and sprinkle with sugar-cinnamon mixture.

Cream Pastries from Belém

Pastéis de Belém follow an ancient "secret recipe" from the monastery of Belém, known exclusively to the master confectioners who baked the pastries, the recipe remained unchanged to the present day. Master-pastry-makers are obliged to sign a "Term of Confidentiality" in order to be accepted in the "secret's room" where the pastries are made.

200g/7oz sugar
4fl.oz. water
1 tsp orange blossom water*
8 egg yolks
500ml/¾ pint cream
1 package puff-pastry dough
Cinnamon and icing sugar
12 custard cups or ramekins

*Orange blossom water can be found at farmers markets, specialty food stores, and Middle Eastern grocers. A little goes a long way, so add it a few drops at a time to determine how much you like.

1. Preheat the oven to 250°C/500°F.
2. Simmer water and sugar until melted and pale like golden syrup. This will take about 6 minutes over moderately low heat.
3. Whisk cream and egg yolk, a bit cinnamon and the orange blossom water into the Syrup stirring and bring very, very gently to the boil. Remove from heat and let cool.
4. Roll puff-pastry well. Cut puff-pastry in small circles and make each fit into the cups using your fingers.
5. Fill the half of each cup with the cream and bake (12 to 15 Minutes) until the pastry is ready and cream gets light burned on the top.
6. Sprinkle with cinnamon and icing sugar. Serve warm or cold.

Sauces

White sauce

2 tbsp butter
1 onion, finely chopped
Freshly ground white pepper
2 tbsp flour
250ml/9fl. oz. milk
250ml/9fl. oz. meat stock or fish stock according to the use of sauce
Salt
¼ tsp freshly grated nutmeg

1. Heat butter in a sauce pan and stir fry onion until softened.
2. Sift flour over onions, stir well until light gold in colour.
3. Pour in milk and stock and stir until sauce thickens.
4. Season with salt, pepper and nutmeg to taste.

Tip
The white sauce should neither be too thick nor too watery.

Cheese sauce

White sauce
100g/3½oz cheese according to taste, grated (Cheddar, Parmesan)
30g/1oz butter
1 egg yolk, beaten

1. Fold cheese, butter and egg yolk into the white sauce.

Butter sauce

This is a simple sauce which goes well with boiled or grilled fish.

125g/4½oz salted butter
2 tbsp margarine
Juice of ½ lemon
Pepper
1 bunch parsley, chopped

1. Cut the margarine into 1cm/½in pieces and put in a sauce pan with the lemon juice. Bring to a simmer, stirring all the time. Do not allow to boil.
2. Stir in butter and parsley, season with pepper and serve immediately.

Cocktail universal sauce

1 tbsp tomato purée
1 tsp of lemon juice
1 tbsp Madeira, very dry or dry sherry
Worcester sauce (molho inglês)
Piri-Piri or chilli sauce
1 cup crème fraîche or cottage cheese
Mayonnaise (if desired)
Salt and pepper

1. Whisk together tomato purée, lemon juice, salt and pepper.
2. Add Madeira or sherry, a dash of Worcester sauce and Piri-Piri to taste.
3. Fold in crème fraîche or cheese and mayonnaise into the mixture.
4. Serve cold with shrimps or vegetables.

Farmer's sauce

2 tbsp vegetable oil
1 tbsp vinegar
½ tsp mustard
Salt and pepper
½ onion, finely chopped
3 bunches parsley, finely chopped

1. Whisk all ingredients together. Serve with salads and roast meat.

Vinaigrette

2 tbsp vegetable oil
2 tbsp vinegar
½ tsp mustard
1 tsp oregano
1 tbsp water
1 tbsp white wine
Salt and pepper

1. Whisk all ingredients together. Serve with salads.

Tip
Create your own vinaigrette with your favourite herbs and more or less vinegar to taste.

Curry sauce

1 tbsp butter
1 onion, finely chopped
1 glass coconut milk
2 tomatoes, peeled, seeded and finely chopped
1 apple, peeled, cored and finely sliced
1 tbsp curry powder
1 tbsp fresh grated ginger root
Piri-Piri or cayenne pepper to taste
1 tsp fresh coriander, finely chopped
200ml/7fl. oz. cream

1. Fry onion in butter.
2. Add curry, ginger, Piri-Piri, apple and tomato, stirring all the time. Bring to a simmer.
3. Deglaze with coconut milk, simmer for a while then add the cream. Do not allow to boil.
4. Strain the sauce through a sieve and sprinkle with coriander.

Butter sauce "Maître d'hotel"

200g/7oz soft butter
2 tbsp chopped parsley
Juice of 1 lemon
Pinch salt

1. Mix butter, salt, parsley and lemon juice well together with a fork.
2. Serve with fish and grilled meat.

Tomato sauce

1 tbsp olive oil or butter
1 onion, finely chopped
1 carrot, peeled and finely chopped
1 bay leaf
1 tsp oregano
1 tbsp celery root, finely chopped
1 can peel tomatoes
Pinch sugar
Pinch salt

1. Heat fat and fry onion, carrot and celery. Add bay leaf and season with salt.
2. Add tomato, oregano and sugar stirring and bring to a simmer. Add some water if necessary and simmer for 20 minutes.
3. Discard bay leaf, purée sauce and simmer for another 10 minutes.

Tip
Use larger quantities of ingredients and prepare some sauce for stock. You can use it when preparing soups, especially tomato soup.